Advance Praise for Alien

Alien is a well thought-out and challenging book. Daryl Driver leads the reader on a path of exploration regarding what it means to live as a citizen of God's Kingdom in the midst of the kingdoms of this world. Daryl works hard to ground his teaching in the Word of God. I believe this is an important work and well worth the time it takes to read it. Thank you, Daryl!

> — Ric Gullman, Pastor of Morning View
> Mennonite Church and Lead Overseer of the
> Mountain Valley Mennonite Churches

In *Alien*, Daryl skillfully and clearly reminds us as the body of Christ, that this is not our home and that there are great rewards for those that follow after the Savior and truly live like it.

> — Lenn Miller, Career Missionary with
> DestiNations International

In his encouraging new book *Alien: Created for Another Kingdom*, Daryl Driver invites us to a biblical vision for navigating a world that is not our home.

> — Delbert Beiler, Leadership Development
> Consultant

Alien

Created For Another Kingdom

Daryl Driver

Word of Grace Ministries

To my incredible wife Kay, for whom, like the grace of God, I grow increasingly thankful each additional year, and for the wonderful children – Tabitha, Bethany, Josiah, Nathan and Gideon – she brought into the world.
Thanks also to the beta readers for this project, who provided feedback and support in a most helpful way.

Contents

1. THE ALIEN CALL 1
   All of Us Want to Belong 2
   The Challenge of Being Alien 4
   Getting the Big Picture 6

2. ALIENATED FROM GOD 8
   Understanding the Journey of Jesus 11
   The Seriousness of Sin 12
   An Illustration of Deterioration 14
   Turning from Our Transgressions 15

3. RECONCILED TO GOD 18
   The Road of Repentance 21
   A Word Toward Wisdom 23

4. ALIEN OF ALIENS 26
   Leaving the Familiar for the Foreign 26
   Having Christ-Centered Priorities 30

5. SEEING CHRIST IN SCRIPTURE 34
   Analyzing the Ark 35
   Remembering Reverence 36
   Symbolizing the Savior 38
   Coming Our Way 38
   Mission of Mercy 40

6. ABRAHAM AND PERSEVERANCE 42
   In Praise of Perseverance 43
   The Power of Ordinary Persistence 44
   Sensing God's Sovereignty 45
   Gaining a Broader View 46
   A Time to Move Forward 47
   Simultaneously Stewards and Sojourners 48
   Tied to Shoelaces 49

7. MOSES AND FLEXIBILITY 51
  One Able to Shift Gears 52
  Hard to Find a Home 52
  Aliens Suffer Affliction 53
  Traveling the Road of Resistance 55
  Discipleship Means Disruption 56

8. RUTH AND STEADFASTNESS 58
  Unexpected Challenges 59
  A Difficult Decision 61
  Relevance for Today 63
  Matching Works to One's Words 64
  Getting the Order Correct 65
  Faithfulness is Not Forgotten 66

9. URIAH AND LOYALTY 68
  Going Deeper in the Story 69
  An Alien Outlook 70
  A Mandate to Be on the Move 71
  Permission is Not Preference 72
  The Call to Continue 73
  Keeping It Current 74
  Tough Times Will Come 76
  Giving the Glory to God 77

10. ATTRIBUTES OF AN ALIEN 79
  Love Over Revenge 79
  Simplicity Over Luxury 82
  Stewardship and Statistics 84
  Faith Over Fear 85
  Desperation and Dependency 86

11. AN ANTI-ALIEN APPROACH 89
  Building at Babel 90
  1. A Common Language 91
  2. A Common Location 94
  3. A Common Goal 95
  The Proper Pursuit 96
  When the Spirit Moves 97

A Tale of Two Sites 98
Motivation and Direction 99
Forsaking the Familiar 101

12. CITIZENS IN THE NEXT AGE 103
A Realization of Rewards 104
Myth #1 – Christians are Not Judged on
Judgment Day 105
Myth #2 – All Christians Receive the Same
Reward for Eternity 107
Myth #3 – Christians are Not to Seek Any
Reward 110
The Lesson of Love 112
The Source of Our Satisfaction 112

About the Author 117

Chapter 1

The Alien Call

I was 14 years old and terrified.

It was the summer before my ninth-grade year. I had decided to switch from a public to a private school, and the class of students I was joining had already spent a year together. In other words, at the Christian school to which I was transferring, I would be a newbie while most of the freshmen were very familiar with each other. I would be searching for an on-ramp into a group that was already chummy and chugging along.

I was trying to quell my fears, however, by remembering that a church friend of mine was already a member of this returning freshman class. I was banking on this relationship, a bond with a boy I hung out with at congregational events and who had shared some of the same interests I did. I was expecting that friendship to guide me through awkward and unfamiliar territory.

Every year the school held an orientation night. The evening before the first day of classes, students and parents showed up and ate watermelon on the lawn. But what was supposed to be an enjoyable social evening for everyone quickly became a disaster for me. My church friend, I soon discovered, had his own clique at school – and he never gave me as much as a glance the whole evening. I remember tears starting and then flowing down my face in the back of the station wagon on the way home.

I felt like a foreigner. I felt disconnected and isolated in a world of already-existing friendships. Sure, folks were nice and polite, but I was out of my element, trying to figure out where I might fit and how to feel good about myself, and trying to establish connections with those already inside the door.

All of Us Want to Belong

In the long haul, when the stakes are high and the risks are great, few of us prefer to be aliens. We like being in our homelands, in the circles that are familiar to us, where people know our names and we're accustomed to the culture and norms that we've learned to appreciate.

Studies support these assertions. Despite all the opportunities for travel and exploration in the United States, 80% of American young adults live within 100 miles of where they grew up.[1] If that's the reality for young adults, what about the entire adult population of Americans? The research says that on average, we live only 18 miles from our mothers.[2]

I've discovered that there are times when virtually everyone feels like they don't belong – we feel like aliens. It's not just you who feels this way when, for example, you tag along to your spouse's extended family gathering or school reunion, or me feeling the way I did as a high school freshman, walking around friendless and forlorn at orientation night. It's all of us at one time or another, and I've repeatedly come across this particular angst in others.

A decade after that dreaded evening of feeling betrayed by my

---

1. https://www2.census.gov/ces/wp/2022/CES-WP-22-27.pdf,   accessed November 2022.
2. https://www.mentalfloss.com/article/73807/average-american-lives-18-miles-their-mom, accessed November 2022.

church buddy the night before high school started, my wife Kay and I finished our formal education in my home area in Virginia and moved to western Oklahoma, where I pastored a rural church. We had entered a community where everybody already knew everybody else, not to mention knowing everybody else's parents and siblings and cousins as well.

Some communities are hard to break into, and this area was one of those. While the congregation I served made every effort to include me and my family, not every pastor in the vicinity had that experience. The shepherd of another church, who also moved into the community from elsewhere, later confided to me, "I've been here 15 years and my congregation still calls me 'the new pastor.'"

The church that I pastored provided many opportunities for connecting, and there were some wonderful individuals who took part in the ebb and flow of congregational life. One woman seemed to have social and relational threads running in every direction. She was one of our core song leaders and her husband was an elder. She was considered outgoing and vivacious, and the couple was warm and engaging in the congregation and in the community. Each of them grew up in the church and came from families considered to be "pillar clans." The husband was part of a successful farm partnership, and she held a supervisory position at the local college. Their involvement and commitment were so strong to the congregation that they were even custodians for our church building.

One day I ran into her in a church hallway. We caught each other up on the latest happenings and suddenly she said, "You know, sometimes I feel like I'm just not part of the inner circle at church." I struggled to not let the shock in my system express itself on my face. As I processed what to say next, I thought to myself, *Sister, if you're not part of the inner circle – then there ain't no inner circle!*

And after serving as a pastor for several decades, and ministering in multiple congregations, I'm convinced that this woman speaks for many, many others. Virtually everyone, occasionally or often, feels left out, alienated, distant from the inner clique. And this woman gives voice to what folks in very different cultures, locations and eras have experienced down through history.

If we're honest, we at times have a fear of booking that one-way ticket into the unknown. We tend to like our tribes and groups, where we find affirmation and a measure of comfort and familiarity.

The Challenge of Being Alien

Aliens are adventurers. We may admire the perseverance of trail blazers like Martin Luther during the European Reformation or Martin Luther King Jr. during the Civil Rights Movement, but it's one thing to read about alien heroes in books or watch them on movie screens. It's something completely different to actually bear the kind of burdens they bore. Many of us don't feel called or equipped to be pioneers in the way that historical figures have been. And, in our modern world, we may have second thoughts about being aliens in the midst of societal and political tsunamis that always seem just around the corner.

Even if we've conquered the fear of adventure in one area of our lives, it may still dominate in another. I've known men who will carry bundles of shingles along the peak of a roof framework or squeeze through the tightest and muddiest of crawl spaces below a house. But for these same men, just the idea of moving to the next county is excruciating – because it seems that everything they know and love is where they grew up.

To step out in faith, we must step into the unfamiliar. And, if we are following Christ, we do well to remember that God is not against us; He is for us. It is He who calls us to be "aliens and temporary residents" (1 Pet. 2:11) for His glory. In fact, God is always preparing to drive back the fear of the unknown for His people – that fear of being the outsider, that fear of walking the stranger's path.

This approach to walking the stranger's path is nothing new for the people of God. In every generation there have been those who "confessed that they were foreigners and temporary residents on the earth. Now those who say such things make it clear that they are seeking a homeland" (Heb. 11:13b-14). As this passage points out, God has a great exchange in mind. He is intent on trading the fallen and failed world which we desperately cling to – the one we've designed for ourselves – for one that is glorious beyond our imaginings – the one He designs for us. "For here we do not have an enduring city; instead, we seek the one to come" (Heb. 13:14). As the writer of Hebrews makes clear, we will never be fully complete until the new age.

At the same time, eternal life, which anticipates that new age, begins when we surrender to Christ. That is to say, eternal life begins in the here and now. And as we turn our lives over to God, He swaps out the flawed strategies we've come up with so that He might lead us down paths of righteousness – roads that turn out to be at times rough and rowdy, yet nevertheless fruitful and fulfilling. The Lord takes us from an earthly focus on our own comfort and self-satisfaction to pioneering for the sake of higher purposes.

Some of us feel secure when we're surrounded by people who believe like we do, talk like we do and dress like we do. But Jesus sends us forth as "sheep among wolves" with a calling to advance the kingdom of God.

It's easy for Christians to adopt an "airlift" mentality when it comes to the pressures and pain of this life. With this approach we expect God to repeatedly rescue us from calamity and chaos. Yet Jesus prays to His Father regarding another way:

"The world hated them because they are not of the world, as I am not of the world. I am not praying that You take them out of the world but that You protect them from the evil one. They are not of the world, as I am not of the world. Sanctify them by the truth; Your word is truth. As You sent Me into the world, I also have sent them into the world" (Jn. 17:14-18).

Getting the Big Picture

What I want to establish in this book is that we're called to be spiritual aliens for the cause of Christ, and the Bible is replete with models and examples of this very lifestyle. Being an alien for God is not some mission bestowed upon wild-eyed, fringe fanatics. Rather, it is part and parcel of a way of living that surrenders and submits to the One who was alien among sinners.

We actually go through four phases in regard to this alien theme. We are at first aliens (in that we're distant from God). Next, we're citizens (of God's kingdom), then aliens (sent back into the world). Finally, we're citizens (in future, eternal glory). Over the course of this book, we'll look at each of these phases in more detail.

By the way, Jesus also experiences shifts. Regarding human history, He is present at the beginning as Agent of creation, and then continues as Citizen and Sovereign in heaven. Then, when the fullness of time is reached, He adopts the role of Sojourner and Alien even while living on earth among His own people, in His own land, on His own planet. He dies the despicable death of an outcast and criminal. He then rises from the dead to reclaim His place of glory and honor beside the Father and, in due course, will oversee the fullest expression of His kingly rule.

Yet don't forget that middle part of Christ's experience. Don't forget that being alien is, mysteriously and miraculously, part of the nature of God. The Lord of the universe, who created mankind and placed us in an idyllic world that we plunged into ruin and desolation, had no moral duty to then intervene. But He is a missionary God. He condescends to the spiritual squalor and deprivation we've manufactured in order to bring justice, peace and goodness – and He does so entirely out of His selfless love.

Being alien means existing in a new country while still maintaining allegiance to the country you call home. As believers in Jesus, we exist in a fallen world while maintaining an allegiance to the kingdom of God. We live in earthly realms, yet take our orders from a heavenly throne.

But before we delve too deeply into the experience of Christ or that of other alien-citizens, we must understand a certain alien existence – the wrong kind of alien existence for humans, an existence we know first-hand all too well.

Chapter 2

Alienated from God

As a young boy I was devoted to comic book heroes like Superman. So, when I saw an ad for x-ray glasses, I eagerly sent off my money with lofty expectations. What the mailman then delivered to my home, however, was an item not much stronger than construction paper with thin lines running up and down the "lenses," supposedly simulating the ability to see through walls.

When it comes to the Christian faith, people also have assumptions about what is actually being considered – and they can be as wrong about Christianity as I was about the x-ray glasses. I've found that unbelievers have several common ways of misunderstanding the faith, and these ways can be presented as three major categories:

1) Code Religion: that is to say, religion of a rulebook. This approach means trying to find religious salvation – seeking to be acceptable to a divine being(s) – or receive other benefits by following all the rules handed down from above. History is littered with gods that demand specific deeds done or offerings made in return for blessing, both spiritual and material. We can see a form of this approach with men and women serving pagan

gods mentioned in the Old Testament such as Baal and Asherah in the hopes of receiving bountiful harvests and childbirth.

This inclination to what is called "works righteousness" is also seen today throughout the earth, with Muslims practicing good deeds, such as the "five pillars," and devotees of Indian religions doing good so as to experience the right karma – roughly translated as "ethical cause and effect." Each of these two major religious groups thus seeks to have it better in a subsequent life, whether that next life involves paradise or rebirth.

But there are also multitudes who claim the name of Christ and yet view their good works as the doorway to heaven upon their death. Therefore, it is no wonder that many non-Christians think of Christianity as another "works-based" religion. This view is vastly different from being acceptable to God, and reaching heaven, by exercising faith in Him – believing that God has provided a way for us to be righteous in His sight.

Here's a quick quiz: Which of the following equations is actually taught in the Bible?

Faith + Works = Salvation

Faith = Salvation – Works

Faith = Salvation + Works

Take a look at Paul's words in Ephesians 2:8-10: "For by grace you are saved through faith, and this is not from yourselves; it is God's gift – not from works, so that no one can boast. For we are His creation – created in Christ Jesus for good works, which God prepared ahead of time so that we should walk in them."

Salvation is "not from works," and therefore, the first equation, Faith + Works = Salvation, is incorrect.[1] We cannot be saved by works no matter how plentiful and how perfect we may imagine our works to be.

The truth is, we're like kids playing baseball too close to the house, and once we've shattered the bay window, we can never

---

1. We could call this view "legalism." In this sense "legalism" refers to the view that one can be acceptable to God through his or her keeping of the law.

put the pieces back together for what once was. Morally, we've marred and scarred our record before the Judge and no amount of good works can purify our list of wrongs. Sin nullifies our mental list of wonderful deeds we think we've accomplished.

Yet even though works cannot produce reconciliation with God, works are necessarily a part of our lives if we have been saved by the Lord, even as Paul says we are "created in Christ Jesus for good works." Therefore, the second equation, Faith = Salvation − Works, proves to be flawed. It is also incorrect.[2] Speaking of those who claim to follow Him, Jesus said: "Every tree that doesn't produce good fruit is cut down and thrown into the fire. So, you'll recognize them by their fruit. Not everyone who says to Me, 'Lord, Lord!' will enter the kingdom of heaven, but only the one who does the will of My Father in heaven" (Mt. 7:19-21).

The final equation is the one the Bible teaches: Faith = Salvation + Works.

Works must follow faith, or the faith is not genuine, even as James says that "faith, if it doesn't have works, is dead by itself" (Jas. 2:17b). God gives us the power to live a righteous life. Peter sums up much of what we're covering here when he writes of the Lord, "For His divine power has given us everything required for life and godliness, through the knowledge of Him who called us by His own glory and goodness" (2 Pet. 1:3).

2) Club Religion: that is to say, belonging to a social group that mouths spiritual dogma on occasion but is, at the core, an avenue for folks to hang around like-minded individuals. Those who participate in this kind of religion, the thinking goes, are really feeding their communal needs and wants, just as people form secular groups for sociological protection and opportunity.

True, many folks grow up in Christian settings, and Christianity, like some other worldviews, usually produces communal

---

2. We could call this view "license." In this sense "license" refers to the view that God provides personal salvation but does not then require the person being saved to obey God in clear and specific ways.

traditions with various customs. But those who truly follow the teachings of Jesus are forming lifestyles that far and away transcend simple groupthink, and transcend whatever community would be the result of that groupthink.

Christianity is always first and foremost a relationship with God before it is a connection with His followers. It is vertical before it is horizontal. Other people or even the church of Jesus do not save the believer – it is only the Son of God Himself who redeems. It doesn't matter what kind of connections you have at a church or how close you feel to those who follow Christ. You must know the Lord yourself.

3) Crutch Religion: For those who can't succeed in life in the "normal" ways, the thinking goes, there is Christianity. For those who are apt to fall into addictive behaviors like drug use, gambling or excessive drinking, or throw themselves into sexual promiscuity, there is religion as either a carrot or a whip to have them act more respectably.

One problem with this perspective is that the one holding it, more often than not, has little understanding of his or her own desperate need for a Redeemer who can cleanse someone morally and spiritually. We must indeed recognize our spiritual weakness in order to come to the foot of Christ's cross, but as we repent and surrender to Him, He makes us spiritually strong. "Blessed are the poor in spirit, because the kingdom of heaven is theirs" (Mt. 5:3).

In much of this, we follow Jesus' perfect example: "In fact, He was crucified in weakness, but He lives by God's power. For we also are weak in Him, yet toward you we will live with Him by God's power" (2 Cor. 13:4).

Understanding the Journey of Jesus

All of this speaks to the incarnation of Christ. The second Person of the Godhead, who from eternity past experienced worship from heavenly beings and unbroken divine fellowship with the

Father and Spirit, took the form of a helpless infant born to poor peasants in a small, oppressed country. He engaged in manual labor, and when His public ministry finally began, it was only a matter of months until He had a target on His back, first by the Jewish officials, then by Roman authorities, who subjected Him to one of the cruelest deaths conceived by the minds of wicked men.

This Man held no public office, controlled no significant budget, had no key worldly connections and finished his earthly existence hanging on a Roman cross. But in the spiritual realm, He became the ultimate Overcomer, and His disciples follow in His steps.

Thus, the key issue with religion in general, and Christianity in particular, is not one of following the right list of dos and don'ts, or socializing with the right people, or acquiring the right religious prop. It is about surrendering to Someone who understands both purity and sacrifice beyond anything we can fathom, who alone is able to fully deliver us from our sinful and selfish ways.

The Seriousness of Sin

In other words, the issue is not whether each of us has a spiritual disease, as the disease is already taking its toll on us. The issue is whether we accept or reject the only remedy.

We must understand that we begin our existence, in the spiritual sense, as foreigners and strangers to God. We are aliens to God because we clutch to our hearts and lives the ways of our carnal homeland, and stubbornly resist conforming to His ways. In fact, ever since humanity rebelled against the Lord in the garden of Eden, history has documented the unrelenting human assault on God's commands, whether it be overt wickedness such as murder, rape and theft, or more subtle transgressions such as lust, envy and resentment.

We often find it easy to critique nations and movements and

point out their wrongdoing, yet it is crucial to also understand that we have succumbed to the enemy not only at a societal level, but also at a personal level. Jesus makes this abundantly clear in the Sermon on the Mount, as He takes some of the Ten Commandments to their logical – and spiritual – outcomes:

"You have heard that it was said to our ancestors, Do not murder, and whoever murders will be subject to judgment. But I tell you, everyone who is angry with his brother will be subject to judgment" (Mt. 5:21-22a). "You have heard that it was said, Do not commit adultery. But I tell you, everyone who looks at a woman to lust for her has already committed adultery with her in his heart" (Mt. 5:27-28).

And even the Ten Commandments speak to the sins of the spirit, as we see in the first and the last of those decrees: "Do not have other gods besides Me" (Ex. 20:3). "Do not covet your neighbor's house. Do not covet ... anything that belongs to your neighbor" (Ex. 20:17). (To covet is to desire for yourself what belongs to someone else.)

Scripture clarifies this attack of ours on holiness: "There is no one righteous, not even one; there is no one who understands, there is no one who seeks God. All have turned away, together they have become useless; there is no one who does good, there is not even one. Their throat is an open grave; they deceive with their tongues. Vipers' venom is under their lips. Their mouth is full of cursing and bitterness. Their feet are swift to shed blood; ruin and wretchedness are in their paths, and the path of peace they have not known. There is no fear of God before their eyes" (Rom. 3:10b-18).

As the Soviet dissident and gulag survivor Aleksandr Solzhenitsyn said, "The line separating good and evil passes not through states, nor between classes, nor between political parties either – but right through every human heart."

Especially as modern Westerners, we tend to look at every area besides the personal moral one to find what seems needed for human fulfillment. When some suggest our greatest flaw is ignorance, we look to education. When some suggest our greatest flaw is poor health, we look to physical fitness. When some suggest our greatest flaw is isolation, we look to psychotherapy. But Scripture is resoundingly clear that our fundamental crisis is one of disobedience to a holy God.

In this way, we are aliens in the worst sense possible – we are separated and estranged from God: "And you were once alienated and hostile in mind because of your evil actions" (Col. 1:21).

Many who give religion some thought assume that God's compassion and mercy mean that He will wink at our rebellion and look the other way when we violate His authoritative commands. But we make such assumptions at our personal peril.

An Illustration of Deterioration

Several years ago, our house was upgraded with a water softener system. Before the new system was installed, the hard water deposits had gradually left whitish stains on cups, containers and coffee pots, but the changes were subtle, and I subconsciously had grown accustomed to the discoloration of a multitude of kitchen utensils.

However, when the water softener system was actually up and running, I couldn't believe how much of a difference it made throughout our house. Glass mugs, for example, that forever had been fuzzy were now coming out of the dishwasher completely clean and transparent. In the bathroom, the shower head nozzles were no longer getting blocked by mineral deposits and now sprayed a full and consistent stream.

Sin often works like those mineral deposits. Early on, the stain seems slight, and we barely notice any difference. Then gradually, over time, they provide a murkiness – better yet, a sleaziness – to everything. Still, however, when we do notice the stains, we tend to think, *Well, that's just how things are; there's not much anybody can do about that.*

We fall in love with our little excursions into sin – gossip or pornography or pride or consumerism or bitterness or complaining – and we easily end up either caught in some strong addiction that we know we can't break, or we've covertly capitulated to sins of the spirit which have subtly but surely taken over our lives.

How does the stain of sin work itself out in practical ways? When we're invited to lead a project at work or church, we want to help the organization – but we're also tainted by a desire to show others how impressive we are, and to receive their acclaim. When we see someone at a social event, we want to go and say hello – but we're also tainted by our desire to hold back because they once slighted us, or because we're defeated by the fear that we'll say the wrong thing. We lean into the impulses of our sinful nature in a million different ways. We come to rationalize our sin. We call our gossip merely informing those who are concerned. We call our resentment righteous indignation. We call our greed looking out for our families.

Turning from Our Transgressions

At the same time, though, when our spiritual makeup is cleansed – just like the plumbing pipes after the water softener is installed – the effects are amazing. The Spirit shows us our rebellion and when we repent, a humbling takes place, and we pinpoint our moral failure for what it really is. We allow divine truth to invade our minds and hearts and we stop lying to ourselves about denying God His rightful place in our choices and habits.

In the first pastorate I served, I preached a sermon on repentance. Then, at the end of the message, my wife and I stood before the congregation and repented of sinful physical activity – some call it "petting" – that we had taken part in before we were married. I then gave an invitation for anyone to come forward and confess sins to the congregation.

After some silent moments, a woman started sobbing in a pew, at first softly. Then all of a sudden, the spiritual dam burst, and there was no longer any veneer of respectability. She gave up pretense in front of 200 other folks and wept openly over her wickedness as though only Jesus was in the room. She made her way to the front of the sanctuary and confessed her sin of stealing money at her workplace. We prayed for this dear lady and ministered to her before a righteous but merciful God.

I've been part of a variety of congregations for more than half a century, taking part in worship services or small group meetings multiple times a week, and yet I've never heard a church group so quiet as that congregation was when that woman confessed her sins.

Looking back, there were aspects of that service we might have done a little differently. But I can say this – the fear of God fell upon that congregation. It's easy to tell ourselves that our pet rebellion is no big deal, but it's another thing to listen to the heartfelt contrition of a sinner wanting Jesus and the cleansing only He can bring. "The one who conceals his sins will not prosper, but whoever confesses and renounces them will find mercy" (Pr. 28:13).

For each of us, our internal moral system needs ongoing cleansing. We need the work of the Holy Spirit to remove all the selfish deposits that sin leaves behind. God sees how we've viewed others as objects for our gratification. God sees how we've been envious of others' abilities. God sees how we've been bitter and unforgiving when people offended us. And it goes on and on.

No matter what challenges you've gone through – and I realize this sounds archaic to many modern Westerners' ears – your greatest problem is personal sin which separates you from a righteous Creator. There's a reason one old-time preacher said, "We must know God as our enemy before we can know Him as our friend" and another said, "They must be slain by the law of God before they can be made alive by the gospel of God!"

In our modern age we don't like to think of ourselves and other humans as sinners – until someone offends us. When people speak evil against us, when people insult us, when people take something that we believe to be ours, then we don't hesitate to know with certainty in our minds that they are in the wrong, whether we use the label "sinners" for them or not.

Someone encountering what the Bible says about our sins against a just Judge – our spiritual apathy, our cowardice, our jealousy, our rage, our overall selfishness – really has only a couple of options. That person can shrug off or throw away the commands of God and believe that the Almighty is a moral tyrant or ethical busybody – and remain exactly the person they were, facing the same end as before: the judgment of a holy God. Or, they can repent of those sins, and repent of their sinful condition altogether, and find joyful cleansing and forgiveness through the sacrifice of Jesus Christ, the blessed Redeemer.

What exactly is repentance? It is changing your mind and heart in a way that changes your life. John the Baptist commanded his listeners: "Produce fruit consistent with repentance" (Mt. 3:8). Our repentance must be more than crocodile tears – it must be genuine. However, receive encouragement in this: As long as we are willing to repent, God is willing to reform and restore and revive.

"Let the wicked one abandon his way, and the sinful one his thoughts; let him return to the Lord, so He may have compassion on him, and to our God, for He will freely forgive" (Isa. 55:7). "For You, Lord, are kind and ready to forgive, rich in faithful love to all who call on You" (Ps. 86:5).

Chapter 3

Reconciled to God

My parents got divorced when I was around 20 years old. They went their separate ways and usually lived in different communities. The years went by, I pastored churches, and my wife Kay and I raised five children.

A full three decades after my parents got divorced, one of our daughters was getting married. She and her future husband informed Kay and me that for the wedding reception there would be several round tables sitting in the center of the church fellowship hall. Each round table was large enough for eight chairs, and Kay and I would facilitate one of those tables, meaning that we could invite six others to sit with us. The natural line of thinking was to invite Kay's parents, my mother and her husband, and my father and his companion to fellowship with us at the reception meal.

I didn't know how my parents would react to the idea of being seated at the same table for an extended time with each other. But Kay and I agreed that the plan explained above made the most sense, and so I trekked off, with some trepidation, to each of my parents in order to inform them of the proposal and get their individual responses. Although they were living in the same community – the area where Kay and I lived as well – my mother and father hadn't seen each other in two decades.

My father agreed to the plan, but it's the conversation I had with my mother that was striking and unforgettable. "Daryl," she said, looking up at me from the learned experience of three-quarters of a century, "we're too old to hold grudges."

My mother has many wonderful qualities. She taught third grade for her professional career, took seriously the responsibility of raising three boys, hosted foster children, taught Sunday school and cooked meals, all while demonstrating consistency, fairness and dignity. But it was those simple words, words trumpeting the message of forgiveness, words full of hope even when forged from the dust and the grime of life in the trenches, that are some of the most beautiful words I've ever heard from the lips of a human being.

They were the words of reconciliation: reconciliation between one person and another.

Before the wedding, elderly family members were ushered into a side room so they could rest before the actual ceremony. My father and mother ended up sitting next to one another. "I'm sorry," said my father to my mother, "that I did many things wrong."

"Well, we also," my mother replied, "did many things right. We have three wonderful sons."

Following the ceremony was the reception meal, with an absolutely therapeutic time of fellowship around that special table that Kay and I headed. There was smiling, there was laughter, there was community. Two aunts and an uncle, the siblings of my mother, came from out of state to the wedding, and at the reception walked over from their table to ours and conversed with my father. And again, whether formally announced or not, reconciliation happened, beautiful to God and to us.

Everyone in my family was stunned at how long my father stayed during the reception. He enjoyed himself and it showed.

Two days later I received a phone call and the treasured

memories from the wedding quickly faded. I had to go to our local hospital as my father had a ruptured hernia.

When my parents divorced, my father had walked away from the church. I'd come to think that even though he was always a part of a Christian congregation up until that time, he never really had a genuine relationship with God. My father was raised by a man who was known in the community, and certainly in his own family, as being legalistically strict. There were challenges my father had, as the oldest son in a family of eight children, that I didn't really understand.

Yet, over the years, my dad mellowed, and became more open to spiritual matters.

At the church I was pastoring during my father's golden years, the man who directed our sound setup told me that while our congregation typically had a good handle on who was calling in to listen to services, a strange phone number was showing up in the records every Sunday morning to tune in.

"I'd like to see that number," I said. Sure enough, it was my father's.

In his twilight years he and I had talked a number of times about the gospel, about what it means to repent of your sins and trust in the person, and the death, and the resurrection of Jesus Christ in order to be saved.

When I walked into my father's hospital room – when he was stricken by the massive hernia – he had tubes running down his throat and couldn't speak. At this point I was aware that physically he had been slowing down in various ways – he had a bout with lymphoma earlier – and now there was a sense that the end was near.

I talked with my father and said, "Dad, you know you have to trust in Jesus." He nodded his head. I prayed with him. And the next day he left this world.

I am certainly aware that I cannot fully dissect and discern anyone's spiritual condition, even my own father's. "Man does not see what the Lord sees, for man sees what is visible, but the

Lord sees the heart" (1 Sam. 16:7b). I cannot know this for sure, but I'd like to think that my father did finish the race, coming not only closer to the kingdom of God, but actually into the kingdom of God.

And if so, that would be the most glorious type of reconciliation: reconciliation between my father, a human being created in the image of God, and his Creator.

"And you were once alienated and hostile in mind because of your evil actions. But now [Christ] has reconciled you by His physical body through His death, to present you holy, faultless, and blameless before Him – and if indeed you remain grounded and steadfast in the faith, and are not shifted away from the hope of the gospel that you heard" (Col. 1:21-23a).

Note carefully Paul's description of our condition before coming to Christ: "alienated and hostile in mind because of [our] evil actions." We considered earlier in this book that we all start out as aliens. We are alienated from God because of our sin – we are sinners by our nature and sinners by our behavior. And it's the depth of our rebellion that necessitates the depth of the needed reconciliation.

The Road of Repentance

Multitudes foolishly think they can negotiate with God, that as lost rebels they can somehow work out a deal toward the end of their days with the Most High. But a drowning man never negotiates his own rescue. Fortunately, the Lord is as merciful as He is holy.

"But God proves His own love for us in that while we were still sinners Christ died for us! Much more then, since we have now been declared righteous by His blood, we will be saved through Him from wrath. For if, while we were enemies, we were reconciled to God through the death of His Son, then how much more, having been reconciled, will we be saved by His life!" (Rom. 5:8-10).

Early in my pastoral career, I preached a sermon about wicked lifestyles and spoke of the end result of such lifestyles – the lake of fire. A young man, who had grown up in the congregation and had regularly received biblical teaching, wanted to see me that week, and so we got together.

In our conversation, he tried to justify a lifestyle completely opposite of the gospel. In my office, he argued that although he was cohabitating with a woman from the community, he was in fine spiritual shape. He wasn't, for example, breaking the seventh commandment, "Do not commit adultery," because she wasn't married to someone else at the time! My response was along the lines of, "You're committing adultery against the Lord! You're claiming to be a follower of Christ, but you're living for yourself rather than for God."

An attitude like the one this young man exhibited stands as a brick wall keeping a person from the kingdom of God. If we want to know the salvation we desperately need from the Lord, we don't come to Him twisting the meaning of Scripture and deceiving our own consciences. We don't try to write our own covenant with the King of glory. Such an approach is an arrogant attempt to think we can alter our record, alter the reality of God's righteousness and alter the retribution we deserve from a fearsome Judge.

"The one who believes in the Son has eternal life, but the one who refuses to believe in the Son will not see life; instead, the wrath of God remains on him" (Jn. 3:36).

Rather than adopting the approach of the young man justifying fornication, we must come to our Judge in genuine repentance and contrition. When we lack these attitudes, the misguided rationalizations we often hold in their place keep us at arm's distance from heaven – and the stakes could not possibly be higher.

One of Jesus' parables clarifies the central importance of deep repentance:

"Two men went up to the temple complex to pray, one a

Pharisee and the other a tax collector. The Pharisee took his stand and was praying like this: 'God, I thank You that I'm not like other people – greedy, unrighteous, adulterers, or even like this tax collector. I fast twice a week; I give a tenth of everything I get.' But the tax collector, standing far off, would not even raise his eyes to heaven but kept striking his chest and saying, 'God, turn Your wrath from me – a sinner!' I tell you, this one went down to his house justified rather than the other; because everyone who exalts himself will be humbled, but the one who humbles himself will be exalted" (Lk. 18:10-14).

The glorious gospel of Jesus Christ is about a transition from a certain kind of alienation to a certain kind of reconciliation – from the kingdom of darkness to the kingdom of light. "So then you are no longer foreigners and strangers, but fellow citizens with the saints, and members of God's household" (Eph. 2:19).

And this transition is possible only because a righteous God is incredibly compassionate.

A Word Toward Wisdom

Let me ask you this question: If you were limited to one word to describe becoming a Christian, which word would it be? "Belief" is a good, biblical word, but in our time it usually conveys intellectual assent, even when that mental agreement with doctrine is not followed up with obedience. "Obedience" is another good, biblical word, but can convey following a list of rules without regard to any transformation of heart that needs to happen beforehand.

The word I would choose is "surrender." To my way of thinking, "surrender" conveys something of the attitude with which we must come to the Savior, penitent and broken, yet also conveys something of the new-found commitment to which we are called in following our Master.

So, from our human side of the equation, we surrender. Next question: What word would we use to describe what happens

from God's side? A good, biblical word that works really well is
"adopt."

Adoption may bring to mind images of lovely new family
connections and children grateful to be cared for by doting
parents. At the same time, those who have been involved in actual
family adoptions know this is often a messy, sometimes excruciating process.

Kay and I are friends to a couple who went through an
emotional roller-coaster experience leading up to their first adoption. Previously they had two potential adoptions that didn't end
with actually retaining a new child. Of course they didn't know
that during those stretches of time; in fact, in both situations they
thought the transfer had happened, but the law in the state where
they were trying to adopt required a waiting period after birth in
which the biological mother – going through an incredibly difficult process herself – could change her mind. And this change of
mind did in fact happen on both occasions for our friends. In one
of those heartbreaking cases, this husband and wife had the baby
in their laps before they received the news that the adoption
would not occur after all.

But as painful as it often was, this couple stayed with the long-
term process – the roller-coaster – and eventually adopted one
baby girl, and then later another one.

This analogy, while not illustrating every nuance of salvation,
hopefully reminds us that spiritual adoption is not some trim and
tidy event. God experiences a kind of travail to bring a sinner into
His kingdom, and to make conversion even possible He called His
own Son to suffer beyond our comprehension: "He made the
One who did not know sin to be sin for us, so that we might
become the righteousness of God in Him" (2 Cor. 5:21).

Through endurance and faithfulness, the Lord ushers us into
His own family, into His own household.

And this adopting work by God was not something He
thought up right before you or I needed it, but is the culmination
of ages of planning and persevering:

But when the completion of the time came, God sent His Son, born of a woman, born under the law, to redeem those under the law, so that we might receive adoption as sons. And because you are sons, God has sent the Spirit of His Son into our hearts, crying, 'Abba, Father!' So you are no longer a slave, but a son; and if a son, then an heir through God" (Gal. 4:4-7).

We were adopted – we are reconciled – not because we were lovable, but because God is loving.

Chapter 4

Alien of Aliens

The Bible presents many spectacular portraits of Christ: Isaiah presents Him as the Suffering Servant, Matthew as the Messiah, and Hebrews as our High Priest and Sacrifice. And here's one more portrait of Christ: Alien. In this chapter we'll explore how Scripture paints this particular profile.

We often think of Christ as the Suffering Servant who hangs on the cross, the Messiah who fulfills Old Testament promises, and the Priest and Sacrifice who takes away the sin of the world – and rightfully so. We are absolutely in need of a sin-bearer and promise-fulfiller who qualifies us to be fully family of a holy God.

But we must also remember what it meant for Him to come to us in the first place. Before He could do the work of redemption, He had to enter and inhabit our ruined world. Before He could travel to the cross of Calvary, He had to travel the roads of Judea and Galilee. Before He could die for us, he had to live with us. To be our Savior, He had to come to foreign territory.

Leaving the Familiar for the Foreign

Christ knew exactly what it was to be alien. He also knew, believe it or not, the feeling of a certain kind of inadequacy. He knew what it was to scan the horizon for visible, tangible results at the end of His journey and see nothing. When He hung on the cross He was aware of one disciple betraying Him, one disciple denying Him and the other disciples forsaking Him. And these were the ones He poured Himself into, the ones in whom He invested all the ministry years of His short life.

Many don't realize the degree to which Scripture records the sense of helplessness and hopelessness, real in the context of an earthly human experience, that He felt at the end of His sorrow-saturated life. One of the most remarkable passages in the Bible is when the Suffering Servant, whom we learn to be none other than Jesus, says in Isaiah 49: "But I myself said: I have labored in vain, I have spent my strength for nothing and futility" (v. 4a).

In His life on earth, Jesus would actually see little of the spiritual fruit from His sacrificial suffering, compared to the investment He made. There was the promise of it, such as Peter proclaiming Him to be the Messiah or the thief hanging beside Him who asked Jesus to remember him. But at the very end, the Lord's own disciples would be sheep who scattered, and the Shepherd was abandoned and abused. And so we see that aliens, who no longer prize creature comforts but are striving for spiritual gain, are destined to feel deep frustration at crucial moments of crisis. They become acquainted with a perspective of foreignness.

Jesus told the Jewish religious leaders: "You are from below ... I am from above. You are of this world; I am not of this world" (Jn. 8:23). Christ says later in the gospel of John: "My kingdom is not of this world" (Jn. 18:36).

In our time, someone speaking the words, "I am not of this world," can conjure up images of otherworldly hovercrafts or extraterrestrial beings.

Christ is from an even more distant place. He came to us from a completely other realm – He arrived at our physical dimension from His spiritual homeland. He came from a location where the will of God is fully obeyed, the glory of God is fully manifested, and the worship of God is fully offered: "Whenever the living creatures give glory, honor, and thanks to the One seated on the throne, the One who lives forever and ever, the 24 elders fall down before the One seated on the throne, worship the One who lives forever and ever, cast their crowns before the throne, and say: Our Lord and God, You are worthy to receive glory and honor and power, because You have created all things, and because of Your will they exist and were created" (Rev. 4:9-11).

Jesus left a land of perfection to arrive in a realm of corruption. He left consummate fellowship with the Father and the Holy Spirit, with no personal need for human entanglement, to come to a world marked by isolation and self-worship and depravity. He went from receiving the rapturous worship of heavenly beings to receiving the torturous treatment of earthly imposters.

The songwriters at times try to capture in words the transition from heaven to earth made by the Son of God with lines like these:

"Christ who left His home in glory"[1]; "Word of the Father, now in flesh appearing"[2]; and then especially at Christmastime we sing:

> *"Christ by highest Heav'n adored*
> *Christ the everlasting Lord!*
> *Late in time behold Him come*
> *Offspring of a Virgin's womb*
> *Veiled in flesh the Godhead see;*
> *Hail the incarnate Deity."*[3]

Jesus gives us the quintessential explanation of His coming to

---

1. Kolb, Abram Bowman. "Christ Who Left His Home in Glory" ("Christ is Risen"). 1896. https://hymnary.org/hymn/CYBER/1136, accessed August 2023.
2. Wade, John Francis (attr.), Frederick Oakeley (trans.). "O Come, All Ye Faithful." 1841 (trans.). https://hymnary.org/text/o_come_all_ye_faithful_joy ful_and_triumph, accessed August 2023.
3. Wesley, Charles. "Hark! The Herald Angels Sing." 1739. https://hymnary.org/text/hark_the_herald_angels_sing_glory_to, accessed August 2023.

our world from His world, with simple but profound language: "The One who comes from above is above all. The one who is from the earth is earthly and speaks in earthly terms. The One who comes from heaven is above all. He testifies to what He has seen and heard" (Jn. 3:31-32a).

Christ is telling us that we, as failed and flawed human beings, need a solution that is beyond our experience and even beyond our universe. We don't need more of the same, "but only better." We don't need a more energetic attempt at political campaigns and strategies. We don't need a flashier attempt at more exciting Christian moviemaking. We don't need a more sensational attempt at catchy, relevant songwriting.

What we need is to know deeply "the hope of His calling, what are the glorious riches of His inheritance among the saints, and what is the immeasurable greatness of His power to us who believe, according to the working of His vast strength" (Eph. 1:18b-19). What we need more of is Jesus – not in some inscrutable, unreachable way, but in fellowship with Him through the Scriptures, through prayer and worship, through the body of Christ, and through obedience in carrying out His kingdom work on earth.

Gregory of Nazianzus, church father of the 300s, summed up much of what we're looking at when he said: "Let us become like Christ, since Christ became like us. ... He assumed the worse that He might give us the better; He became poor that we through His poverty might be rich; He took upon Him the form of a servant that we might receive back our liberty; He came down that we might be exalted; He was tempted that we might conquer; He was dishonored that He might glorify us; He died that He might save us ..."

John the Baptist, who knew a thing or two about being a spiritual alien, said it this way of Christ: "He must increase, but I must decrease" (Jn. 3:30).

Having Christ-Centered Priorities

To be clear, regarding my earlier comments, I'm not against Christians voting, Christians making movies or Christians recording music. I vote and absorb Christian media myself.[4] But those involvements and others like them are absolutely, positively secondary engagements for kingdom-focused believers. Christ is not waiting to return until we've created the perfect Christian presidential ballot or the perfect Christian movie. Rather: "This good news of the kingdom will be proclaimed in all the world as a testimony to all nations. And then the end will come" (Mt. 24:14).

We don't need more of the same of what this world offers, only infused with some religious taglines or Christianized in some way. To head in the right direction, we must absorb the truth that Jesus is not from below – He is emphatically from above.

Paul said it this way: "The first man [Adam] was from the earth and made of dust; the second man is from heaven" (1 Cor. 15:47).

True, we bear the likeness of the Father. The Lord has made us in His image. But we humans love to return the favor and try to make Him in ours. That is to say, we imagine, despite the consistent teaching of Scripture, that Jesus is from below – that He is really like us, after all.

Some love to fashion Jesus as a communist activist who did nothing but champion social liberation for various oppressed groups. But Christ had abundant opportunity to show those colors if they had truly been His. For instance, when He visited a home in the town of Bethany:

> As He was reclining at the table, a woman came with an
> alabaster jar of pure and expensive fragrant oil of nard. She broke

---

4. Actually, I've tried my hand at writing a song to capture something of the faithfulness of Christ. At the back of the book you can find *There is Jesus*.

the jar and poured it on His head. But some were expressing indignation to one another: 'Why has this fragrant oil been wasted? For this oil might have been sold for more than 300 denarii and given to the poor.' And they began to scold her" (Mk. 14:3-5).

To this Jesus responds, "You always have the poor with you, and you can do good for them whenever you want, but you do not always have Me. She has done what she could; she has anointed My body in advance for burial. I assure you: Wherever the gospel is proclaimed in the whole world, what this woman has done will also be told in memory of her" (Mk. 14:7-9).

For many who present Christ as a progressive icon, this account is problematic, as Jesus clearly places a spiritual priority (His presence and His sacrifice) above a material priority (helping the poor). The account becomes understandable once we realize that Jesus believed His death accomplished what a king's treasury could never attain for men and women – their salvation from sin.

The Son of Man did not come to be served, but to serve, and to give His life – a ransom for many" (Mt. 20:28). "We plead on Christ's behalf, 'Be reconciled to God.' He made the One who did not know sin to be sin for us, so that we might become the righteousness of God in Him" (2 Cor. 5:20b-21).

In a similar way, some want to fashion a Jesus who meshes with modern Western causes of extreme animal rights and ultra-environmentalism. Yet, according to the biblical record, He placed His own ministry and what it represented far above the value He placed on animals – His deliverance ministry once caused the drowning of roughly 2,000 pigs. Additionally, He placed His teachings far above the value He placed on plants – to create a visual aid, He once withered a fig tree from the roots upward.

Nor did Jesus' ministry ever excuse sin as nothing more than an unavoidable human characteristic. Those who fashion Jesus as a harmless hippie winking at their immorality conveniently ignore His repeated warnings about where masses will spend the afterlife: "The Son of Man will send out His angels, and they will gather from His kingdom everything that causes sin and those guilty of lawlessness. They will throw them into the blazing furnace where there will be weeping and gnashing of teeth" (Mt. 13:41-42). He spoke unsparingly of "hell, where their worm does not die, and the fire is not quenched" (Mk. 9:48).

Then on the other side of the political and religious fence, there are voices who love to portray Jesus as a gun-toting, flag-saluting good ol' boy who delighted in spreading capitalist doctrine. He failed to live up to this stereotype as well. Once again, Christ had repeated opportunities to promote this kind of popular cause – in this case, for example, defending oneself and one's group with arms – but did not.

When the mob came to arrest Him at the Garden of Gethse-mane, He could have supported the use of weaponry by Peter, and thus by extension the use of weapons by other disciples down through the centuries. Instead, however: "Jesus told [Peter], 'Put your sword back in place because all who take up a sword will perish by a sword'" (Mt. 26:52).

Similarly, we read this response when Christ was questioned by Pilate: "'My kingdom is not of this world,' said Jesus. 'If My kingdom were of this world, My servants would fight, so that I wouldn't be handed over to the Jews. As it is, My kingdom does not have its origin here'" (Jn. 18:36).[5]

It's easy for us to proclaim strong commitment to Christ

---

5. It's just possible that Jesus also referred to not attaching oneself tightly to earthly cliques when He said in Lk. 9:58b that "the Son of Man has no place to lay His head." From this perspective Jesus would be speaking metaphorically. The context Luke establishes in this section includes Jews being taught not to condemn Samaritans (9:52-56), and disciples taught not to attach too tightly to family (9:59-60) or "those at my house" (9:61-62). In 9:50 Christ says: "... whoever is not against you is for you." The parallel passage in Matthew does not have most of these features but the man prompting Jesus to make His "no place" comment is categorized as part of a socioreligious group: the scribes.

while cultivating and isolating our hand-picked interpretations of limited passages regarding Jesus's life and teachings. But we are wholly obligated to conform ourselves to Christ in every area of life – how we relate to those around us, how we deal with money, how we handle sexuality, how we find mutual support and accountability in Christ's church, and on and on. How easy it is to forget that the Great Commission at the end of Matthew's gospel contains these words of Jesus: "teaching them to observe everything I have commanded you" (Mt. 28:20).

Are there teachings and disciplines given by Jesus that you secretly (or not so secretly) want to avoid? Are you willing to put into practice the way of Christ even when it flies in the face of your chosen political party or religious community? Simply put, is Jesus the Lord of every aspect of who you are?

Chapter 5

Seeing Christ in Scripture

A little girl often visited an elderly woman who lived across the street. This widow served as a stand-in grandmother, offering cookies and milk to the girl despite a very limited budget. On a visit when she was maybe seven years old, the girl brushed up against a ceramic figurine, knocking it to the floor where the head broke off. The girl was horrified, but the woman simply picked it up, told her it didn't matter and gave her a big hug. The widow said that the girl's visits were more valuable to her than any of her possessions.

The girl was amazed. The next time she found herself in the widow's house, she noticed the figurine back in its usual spot, head firmly glued in place.

Years later, after the widow had died, her children had an estate sale at her home. The girl who had visited so often was now a young lady, and she attended the sale to find something to remember her friend by. When she walked inside, the young lady caught sight of the little figurine and her eyes became misty. She knew no one would ever appreciate that ceramic piece as much as she would, and so she purchased and forever prized a keepsake that spoke more than words.

When we consider the long-term impact of the figurine upon

the young lady, we realize that this little ceramic piece served a purpose beyond its more obvious intended use. A powerful symbol, it reminded the young lady of mercy and forgiveness neither deserved nor expected – of compassion that has an origin from above.

The figurine symbolically points to something greater than itself. And in similar fashion, God gives us symbols in Scripture that point to Christ. Scholars speak of "types," and the persons or objects existing before Jesus, yet serving as symbols of Him, are types of Christ. These Old Testament symbols point to, and teach us about, the Lord.

Many biblical heroes are types of Christ. Isaac, whose father Abraham was willing to offer as a sacrifice, is a type of Christ. Joseph, who was rejected by his brethren yet exalted by God after his humiliation, is a type of Christ. Moses, a deliverer for the people of God and mighty in word and deed, is a type of Christ.

And to this list of symbols for Jesus let us add an object: the ark of the covenant.

Analyzing the Ark

The ark of the covenant, also called the ark of the Lord, was a wooden chest designated by God to be the central piece of the tabernacle, an area bordered by a courtyard fence and featuring a tent made of wood and metal framing with various coverings.

The tabernacle served as a center of sacrifice and worship for the Israelites, but was not static like the temple, its eventual replacement. The tabernacle was mobile – and the ark was even more mobile than the tabernacle. In fact, the ark was *alien*, ready to travel into enemy territory for divine purposes.

Let's look at three Old Testament accounts that begin to give us a potent picture of how the ark of the covenant functioned among God's people.

First, there is the battle at Jericho, where God instructed Israel to invade and conquer a strongly fortified city. The plan called for the Israelites to march once daily around Jericho for six days, then "on the seventh day, march around the city seven times, while the priests blow the trumpets. When there is a prolonged blast of the horn and you hear its sound, have all the people give a mighty shout. Then the city wall will collapse, and the people will advance, each man straight ahead" (Josh. 6:4b-5).

Interestingly, when the forces of God completed the initial trip around the city on the first day, the record does not say: "And the Israelites circled the city." What it says is: "So the ark of the Lord was carried around the city" (Josh. 6:11a). The ark led the people of God, who experienced victory with the unfolding of His plan. While the Lord sought – and seeks – to spiritually lead His people on the journey of life, the ark physically led the Israelites, in corresponding fashion.

Remembering Reverence

For the Israelites, the danger with an item like the ark was to lapse into thinking of it as a good-luck charm or magical toy. Tragically, the Old Covenant people of God did exactly that and learned this lesson the hard way. They lived lives distant from the Lord and instead of repenting of their sin, decided to put their trust in the ark instead of the One the ark represents. And this truth brings us to the second incident:

The Philistines captured the ark at a low point in Israel's history, and imagined that they would then have the upper hand. But they suffered their own divine judgment while housing the item. Therefore, they ended up sending it back on a cow-driven cart to Israelite territory. Yet even after all this, the Israelites still had not developed a healthy fear of the Lord and a commitment to His commands:

> God struck down the men of Beth-shemesh because they looked inside the ark of the Lord. He struck down 70 men out of 50,000 men. The people wept because the Lord struck them

with a great slaughter. The men of Beth-shemesh asked, 'Who is able to stand in the presence of this holy Lord God? Who should the ark go to from here?'" (1 Sam. 6:19-20).

And finally, the third incident: Sometime after this tragedy occurred among his people, David attempted to bring the ark to his own home. But again, Israel experienced sorrow as Uzzah ignored God's decrees regarding how the sacred ark was to be handled, and when he touched the symbol of the Lord's presence with his own hand, he immediately paid for it with his life.[1]

Despite the travail and agony that Israel experienced during these days, the outcome for those who truly feared God and respected His laws could be radically different concerning the ark. One man and his household experienced rich blessing, as seen when David "took [the ark] to the house of Obed-edom the Gittite. The ark of the Lord remained in his house three months, and the Lord blessed Obed-edom and his whole family" (2 Sam. 6:10b-11).

Through these accounts, we picture the presence, the power and the patience of God. We learn that the ark – representing the Lord Himself – should be followed, feared and favored. The ark of God, although an alien object ready to travel for the Israelites' benefit and blessing, is not a toy at their beck and call. The sojourning ark advances the people's welfare, but is never subject to their whims.

And so it is with the Lord Himself. God is not waiting behind the counter at customer service or sitting at the phone for client assistance. He is reigning in the heavens, possessing incomprehensible power, glory and honor. He owes no one anything – not now, not in the past, not in anyone's future. He is eternal, He is transcendent, He is utterly beyond all else.

---

1. See 2 Sam. 6:1-10.

Symbolizing the Savior

Earlier I stated that the ark represents Jesus. What are further indications of the ark symbolizing Christ?

Jesus is the way, the truth and the life (Jn. 14:6a), and the ark of the covenant represents all of these features. The writer of Hebrews says that inside the ark were "a gold jar containing the manna, Aaron's rod that budded, and the tablets of the covenant [with the Ten Commandments]" (Heb. 9:4b).

Christ as the way is represented by the manna, needed each day on the journey through the wilderness. Christ as the truth is represented by the tablets, which contain the word of God. Christ as the life is represented by Aaron's rod, which twice transformed into something living. The ark is a type of Christ.

At all times, the ark is prepared to be alien. The Bible tells us how the ark routinely led the Israelites in their wanderings: "They set out from the mountain of the Lord on a three-day journey to seek a resting place for them, with the ark of the Lord's covenant traveling ahead of them for the three days. Meanwhile, the cloud of the Lord was over them by day when they set out from the camp. Whenever the ark set out, Moses would say: Arise, Lord! Let Your enemies be scattered, and those who hate You flee from Your presence. When it came to rest, he would say: Return, Lord, to the countless thousands of Israel" (Num. 10:33-36).

Even when resting in the tabernacle, the ark was prepared for travel: "Insert the poles into the rings on the sides of the ark in order to carry the ark with them. The poles are to remain in the rings of the ark; they must not be removed from it" (Ex. 25:14-15).

Coming Our Way

Now when we consider that God is perfectly content to have his ark ready to roam, instead of fixed in a fine cathedral, that may sound strange to our ears. But this is a pattern for God. He does

not wait in finery and luxury for us to claw our way up to Him –
an impossibility in any case – but He stoops down to reach us.
Remember, this is the same God who had His Son born to peasants and laid in a feeding trough for animals!

Even as God demonstrated His humility with the lowly and
meek arrival to earth of His own Son, He demonstrated this
humility long before the coming of Christ with the alien nature of
the ark, which points to the Lord's presence.

The ark is a traveling ark, and our God is a missionary God.
The Lord said to David: "Are you to build a house for Me to live
in? From the time I brought the Israelites out of Egypt until today
I have not lived in a house; instead, I have been moving around
with the tabernacle tent. In all My journeys with all the Israelites,
have I ever asked anyone among the tribes of Israel, whom I
commanded to shepherd My people Israel: Why haven't you built
Me a house of cedar?" (2 Sam. 7:5b-7).

Since earthly kings show their eminence by compelling
subjects to travel to the royal palace, then yes, we might initially
expect the God of the universe to insist His servants come to
Him. Yet, amazingly, the very ark of the Lord travels here and
there, willing to leave a permanent site of dignity and majesty in
order to demonstrate God's readiness to descend to our level and
deliver us from bondage.

In the Bible we see a definite intention on the part of God to
pursue the person in need. When the shepherd in Jesus' parable,
as recorded in the gospels, loses one of his 100 sheep, he goes
looking for the missing lamb. When the prodigal son is heading
back to his family home, the father runs to greet and receive him.
And so when God sent his Son into the world, Jesus was simply
following the pattern of his Father. God walked into the garden of
Eden after mankind sinned. Adam and Eve had to hide themselves
because they knew God *would be coming to them*. When they did
wrong, He pursued them and "investigated," with their best interests in mind.

Mission of Mercy

We, likewise, are called to be alien in representing the right-eousness and the compassion of the one true God, no matter where He sends us. "But thanks be to God, who always puts us on display in Christ, and spreads through us in every place the scent of knowing Him. For to God we are the fragrance of Christ among those who are being saved and among those who are perishing. To some we are a scent of death leading to death, but to others, a scent of life leading to life" (2 Cor. 2:14-16a).

Being like Christ, living out the example of the "missionary" ark, means going the extra mile to demonstrate Jesus to the world around us. Decades ago, our young family moved into an apart-ment building in Columbus, Ohio, greatly assisted by friends from our congregation. The day turned out wonderfully for our move – but not for another couple, whom I'll call Ron and Roxanne. They moved into the same building on the same day – but hours later, when things were not so rosy.

After sunset, as our family was securely settled into our first-floor apartment unit, Ron, Roxanne and their baby girl arrived to move into a second floor unit. We had a multitude of hands helping with our move, and they had ... no one. And then it quickly started to rain.

My wife, busy corralling our three very young children, looked at me and said, "You really ought to help them move in." I remember my sinful nature whispering to me that maybe they didn't desire my help – but really, I couldn't argue with Kay. The whole point of our living in that apartment, and in that city, was to demonstrate the way of Christ to a needy world, which, to my embarrassment now, I was then conveniently forgetting.

So, I asked Ron if he needed help, which he was glad to receive. And then the skies absolutely poured.

However, that was the beginning of a relationship between our households. Later on, after Kay got plugged into a church Bible study with two other women, she wondered about asking

Roxanne to join, but knew she came from a non-Christian background.

Although Kay expected her to reject the invitation, Roxanne's response was: "That's exactly what I need!" At her first Bible study, Roxanne broke down and said to the other women, "This meeting is just what I've been looking for!"

I wish I could say that Roxanne, in short order, surrendered to Christ. Actually, she attended the study a few times and then drifted away. Her duties with first one child and then before long two, and challenges in her relationships, served as obstacles. However, Kay was very much available for her. She was that "fragrance of Christ" that we saw Paul write about to the Corinthians. And that's part of our calling as believers.

"The Son of Man has come to seek and to save the lost" (Lk. 19:10). When we are united with Jesus, we are united with His mission. And His mission is with tax collectors and prostitutes, with arrogant Pharisees and clueless fishermen. His mission – our mission – is investing in people outside the kingdom of God, even though those persons may seem so far distant that we'd think they'd never arrive. We can't dictate outcomes, but we can provide opportunity.

Let me ask you now: Are you willing to leave that cozy couch, those cozy friendships, that cozy day off that you had saved for yourself, to minister to somebody who needs to know and experience more of Christ? Are you willing to get involved with that person who is not as polite, or as neat, or self-disciplined, or as careful with money as you would like, for the sake of God's kingdom? Does your sense of discipleship only involve doing what feels good to you and what results in positive feedback from others – or does it involve going after lost sheep, as messy and complicated as they often are?

Chapter 6

Abraham and Perseverance

S hakespeare wrote, "Some are born great, some achieve greatness, and others have greatness thrust upon them." Abraham is clearly in the last category. When you start to study what various Old Testament giants are known for, he can seem rather out of place alongside these other "Mount Rushmore" figures. With Abraham there's no parting of the Red Sea as with Moses, there's no slaying of the giant as with David, there's no conquering of the heathen prophets as with Elijah.

The writer of Hebrews gives this skeleton overview of the patriarch's life: "By faith Abraham, when he was called, obeyed and went out to a place he was going to receive as an inheritance; he went out, not knowing where he was going. By faith he stayed as a foreigner in the land of promise, living in tents with Isaac and Jacob, co-heirs of the same promise. For he was looking forward to the city that has foundations, whose architect and builder is God" (Heb. 11:8-10).

We could say Abraham's greatest achievement was moving from one place to another, which sounds incredibly ordinary. But with his particular set of circumstances, and with how God guided human history, Abraham turns out to be the prototypical alien. He pioneers what it means to leave one's comfort zones. He did this literally – that is to say, he did it physically – and he did it spiritually.

In Praise of Perseverance

Abraham was called by God to leave his homeland and go to a foreign territory, and later to believe that a child of the promise would come, and he persevered to demonstrate what some 20th century writers have termed "a long obedience in the same direction."

Abraham and Sarah remind us that God is not only at work in the dramatic events of larger-than-life characters, such as calming storms or healing the blind. God is also at work in a husband and wife plodding across the wilderness and waiting patiently (most of the time) for a miracle child to arrive.

We are quick to acknowledge that God is at work if a believer powerfully leads someone to put their trust in Christ, or if a believer receives financial provision out of nowhere to pay that bill at the midnight hour. But the Lord is also accomplishing His will if you teach the next generation one simple lesson of what it means to walk with God, or you dutifully give your tithes and offerings on a regular basis. In other words, discipleship regularly consists of ordinary obedience.

During my seminary days I served as a pastoral intern in my home church. Once I went with an older pastor for nursing home visitation and we came upon an elderly Christian sister who raised a passel of children, including four ordained sons. These men preached the Word of God, guided congregations, wrote note-worthy books and held key roles in Christian higher education.

By the time of this visit I had realized that parenting is not some automatic process where we can guarantee certain results, but I still wanted to take advantage of this singular opportunity to glean wisdom. So, I asked this dear lady something like, "You had a number of children involved in important Christian ministry. How did this work itself out? How did you play a part in so many lives being impacted?"

I'll never forget her answer. She looked at me and said simply, "I washed a lot of dishes, and I prayed a lot of prayers."

With her response, she offered no magic formula, no secret to scaling the Mount Everest of Christian accomplishment. She was saying simply that, by God's grace, she experienced "a long obedience in the same direction." She served and blessed her family in material ways – for example, washing dishes – and she served and blessed them in spiritual ways – for example, interceding before God's throne.

This woman's contributions were of the everyday variety: seemingly trivial, and at times rather boring. And those are precisely the moments and the events that God uses to advance the kingdom of His dear Son.

The Power of Ordinary Persistence

As Westerners, we think that success is determined by numbers and followers and popularity and money. As moderns, we get caught up in whether we are making a splash on social media or have become renowned in our field. But biblically, the critical element is not how famous we are on earth, but how appreciated we are in heaven.

Never underestimate how God can use the ordinary, repetitious events in your life. That children's lesson where every kid's attention seems a million miles away, that plate of cookies you took to a family battling illness, that short conversation with a neighbor at a ball game – you simply don't know how the Lord of glory might use that little nugget to impact an individual next week, or next month, or even a decade later. When our lives are daily submitted to the Lord, He can use little moments in momentous ways.

Toward the end of 2012, my wife and I, living in Virginia's

Shenandoah Valley, decided to distribute plates of goodies and friendly notes on Christmas cards to neighbors on our street. The cards concluded with the words, "Blessings to you! If there's anything we can pray about for you, let us know!"

Kay baked, and I delivered these seemingly insignificant packages on December 12. Two days later our nation recoiled in horror at the Sandy Hook Elementary School killings in Newtown, Connecticut. In short order, 20 children, six staffers, the gunman's mother and the gunman himself had their lives abruptly and tragically ended.

The very next day, one of the families receiving our goodies put a note in the mail which quickly reached our box. It read in part, "Newton, Ct. was our home for 21 years and our children attended school there [not at Sandy Hook, but in that same community]." This connection between our Virginia neighbors and Newton, Connecticut, was completely unknown to us.

The note went on to say that this family still had friends in the Newton area with whom they kept in touch. They ended their note to us by saying, "We ask you to remember the parents of these young victims in your prayers. We want to thank you for your gift, and this is the second time you have reached out to us. Thanks."

I wrote a response note and sent it back through the mail along with a gospel tract.

Sensing God's Sovereignty

Before carrying out a project like distributing small gift packages, or mailing the follow-up gospel tract, it would be easy to say, "Well, it's just a small plate of treats. Well, it's just a card. Well, it's just a tract."

Maybe. But our family handed out those simple gifts, it just so happened, two days before the tragic shootings. And a box of gospel tracts was special delivered to our house, it just so happened, a day before I was wanting to put a tract in the mail for our neighbors.

We serve a God who is in the business of making things "just so happen." Someone might say, "Well, aren't there many events that happen in life that are not tied to national tragedies or something dramatic?" Of course. But as we go about our days, we often perceive such a small sliver of how God is sovereignly orchestrating details for His purposes and for His glory. The Lord desires to broaden our perspective.

As servants of the Lord, we are not responsible for tangible results from our service, but only for hearing and heeding His nudges and promptings. The vast majority of our faithfulness in life will look mundane.

Gaining a Broader View

And just as we dare not expect too much, too soon of our own earthly impact, we also dare not expect too much of the lives of biblical heroes. We must avoid an unhealthy idealism in that regard. We must remember that the faith of Abraham and Sarah is persevering – but it is not perfect.

We do well to remember how Abraham *yielded Sarah* to the control of a foreign king – twice! And in between those two events Abraham *yielded to Sarah* and fathered Ishmael in conjunction with his wife's slave, Hagar. And Sarah, for her part, hearing from the Lord how she would have a son in her old age, laughed at the mention of it. Yet, after earlier recording those flaws of this husband and wife, Scripture has the boldness to say that Abraham "did not waver in unbelief at God's promise" (Rom. 4:20a) and that Sarah "considered that the One who had promised was faithful" (Heb. 11:11c).

True, followers of God at times make choices based on flawed thinking or strong emotions. Yet God in His loving wisdom weighs our lives in the broader context of our overall obedience. He notices those moments of carnality – and responds in His righteousness and discipline – but nevertheless sees it alongside whatever persistent allegiance we've displayed. He graciously looks at the long term.

To be clear, I'm not suggesting that it's okay to live sloppy lives or to be unconcerned about holiness. Abraham and Sarah, and later Moses and David, all paid significantly at times for their acts of disobedience. What I am saying is that we must not hold ourselves to such a high standard that we regularly propel ourselves into despair.

A Time to Move Forward

"But one thing I do: forgetting what is behind and reaching forward to what is ahead, I pursue as my goal the prize promised by God's heavenly call in Christ Jesus" (Php. 3:13b-14). Part of what is "behind" that we must forget are our failures and flaws.

Yes, it's important at times to acknowledge our sins and short-comings. Yet even then, we must discern between the work of the enemy and the work of the Father. Satan condemns, God convicts. What's the difference between the two? Condemnation never offers a path forward or any solution. It tells you, "You've messed up so badly that God will forever reject you." Conviction tells you, "You've sinned; go to God in repentance and humility, and He will restore you – and He longs to do this work of restoration."

When we examine the lives of biblical characters we're trying to strike a realistic balance. And despite his errors, Abraham made many "little" decisions that give us a window into his faith. For example, when he allows Lot to choose which land to live and operate within, we find Abraham demonstrating an "alien mentality" while Lot demonstrates a "settler mentality." Lot, as Abraham's nephew, should have deferred to his uncle when it came to the choice of land, but Abraham's grasp was not on this world's territory or treasures, even though he was a wealthy man.

Furthermore, God's original command to Abraham was to

"Go out from ... your relatives" (Gen. 12:1). As mentioned, Lot
was Abraham's nephew. Thus, with the two men parting ways,
Abraham was finally embracing the full alien approach that the
Lord commanded. And God rewarded Abraham for both his willingness to defer to Lot and his willingness to depart from Lot.

Simultaneously Stewards and Sojourners

Consider further the issue of land ownership in the Old Testament. Abraham, as a nomadic herdsman, never actually owned
the land he made use of, and as herdsmen do, he traveled when
needful. Thus, he continues to fit into the alien category.

However, going further in the historical account of the
Israelites, one could argue that the alien theme disappears. "Sure,"
one could say, "it's true that Abraham was a prototypical alien
before his descendants took over the Promised Land, and Jesus
could be an alien afterward, but the whole point of the Israelites
claiming the land was to occupy and settle there."

But wait just a minute. We have to keep in mind that the law
clearly taught that the Israelites, when they did settle and farm,
were to be *stewards* of the land. This was clear from the
commandment that property could not be permanently sold:
"The land shall not be sold in perpetuity, for the land is [M]ine.
For you are strangers and sojourners with [M]e" (Lev. 25:23,
ESV).

Let's apply this verse by first noticing the last sentence in
Leviticus 25:23. Here's a phrase that is easily overlooked, but is
massive in its impact. God is telling His people that they are
"strangers and sojourners" with Him! Israelite farmers were to see
themselves as aliens with the Lord. In a sense, even God Almighty
was not completely settled in the Promised Land because of the
reality of sin and rebellion against his rule. And the Israelites, even
after making their home in Canaan, were to view themselves as
aliens with God.

If the Israelites carried out the specific teachings of the Mosaic

Law, families would not be able to amass more and more land unto themselves. Individuals would be stewards and caretakers of the property that they managed during their lifetimes. Every fiftieth year, the year of Jubilee, the land was to revert back to the ancestral owners. This means that if you bought additional land – land beyond the boundaries of your ancestral property – you were leasing that property until the fiftieth year. God's law instructed the Israelites to keep a loose hold even on the ground beneath their feet.

Tied to Shoelaces

During my college years, I was part of a Christian ministry team that spent several weeks in Jamaica. As we were preparing to fly back home, I packed my things and decided, considering the incredible affluence of my homeland and the poverty of where I was visiting, the least I could do would be to leave a pair of sneakers for somebody in Jamaica to utilize.

As I took one more look around the room, my eyes fixed on the laces attached to the shoes I was donating. *You know*, I thought to myself, *I could make use of those shoelaces at home*, and without any more processing, removed the laces from the sneakers and stuck them in my suitcase.

It was only as the airplane was soaring over the Atlantic Ocean, did I realize the colossal and absurd nature of my decision. What was I thinking? How expensive are shoelaces in the United States? How miserly could I actually be? I'm embarrassed every time I remember this account.

And yet, truth be told, all of our earthly possessions are of the same caliber as those lowly laces. "But the Day of the Lord will come like a thief; on that day the heavens will pass away with a loud noise, the elements will burn and be dissolved, and the earth and the works on it will be disclosed. ... all these things are to be destroyed in this way" (2 Pet. 3:10-11a).

If you have committed yourself to Christ's command to be a

spiritual alien, what are you hanging onto that could greatly bless someone in need? What will you carry in your possession to the throne of Judgment that will look like shoelaces in your suitcase over the Atlantic? How can you release resources for the advancement of the kingdom of God, for the glory of God?

These are the kinds of questions an alien asks.

Chapter 7

Moses and Flexibility

R eceiving no education beyond the fourth grade, a youngster toiled during four of his teenage years in an industry that increasingly appealed to him. At 18 years of age, he started his own outfit in Philadelphia. However, it ended in bankruptcy. He started another business in New York City. It also ended in bankruptcy. He attempted a third company, this time in central Pennsylvania, and succeeded using innovations he developed during the years of his previous grit and labor.

But even as he finally found success, the young businessman wasn't satisfied. He had his eye on manufacturing a different, but related product. He took a calculated risk, sold his valuable company and started another one. This new venture, guided by trial and error, prospered much more than the previous one.

Married for some time now, the businessman and his wife had been unable to bear children. They channeled their disappointment into starting and funding a school for orphans. In fact, he steered much of his business profits into the town growing around his factory, adding resources in transportation, education and recreation to a community designed to have well-paid workers living with their families in modern homes. "One is only happy," he said, "in proportion as he makes others feel happy."

The town? Hershey. The business? Chocolate. The man?
Milton.

One Able to Shift Gears

Milton Hershey was nothing if not adaptable. His flexibility was a
key component to his amazing success. And these traits of
Hershey's bring to mind another trailblazer, one of the giants of
God's people: Moses, founder of the Old Covenant.

In the previous chapter we studied Abraham. While the father
of the faithful was called to forsake one society for another –
leaving Ur to live in the Promised Land – Moses spent significant
moments of his life shuffling between two cultures: that of Egypt
and that of Israel. Moses knew what it was to be adaptable and
flexible.

Raised by Pharoah's daughter, and thus having access to
Egypt's elite top tier, Moses at the same time was fully Israelite by
birth. Moses was handed the challenge of seeking to adjust to
whatever setting he found himself in at the time.

At first glance, if anyone would seem to be comfortable in
multiple cultures – and thus to insulate himself from an alien
experience – it might appear to be Moses. But as it turned out,
this man of God demonstrates a profound alien ability, as he is
tasked with straddling two worlds and eventually liberating the
people of God from a land of bondage.

Hard to Find a Home

Missionary kids, also classified as third culture kids, at times know
the experience of feeling foreign in two cultures – that of their
parents from the sending country, and that of their adopted land,
the receiving country. Moses was also a man without a nation. He
frequently felt unwanted and unwelcomed by both societies.
When he took time to describe himself, he declared: "I have
become a stranger in a foreign land" (Ex. 2:22b). Moses in fact

ends up being one the greatest examples of an alien in all of Scripture.

When it came to interacting with his kindred Israelites, Moses "assumed his brothers would understand that God would give them deliverance through him, but they did not understand. ... he showed up while [two Hebrew men] were fighting and tried to reconcile them peacefully, saying, 'Men, you are brothers. Why are you mistreating each other?' But the one who was mistreating his neighbor pushed him away, saying: Who appointed you a ruler and a judge over us? Do you want to kill me, the same way you killed the Egyptian yesterday?" (Acts 7:25-28).

This rejection of Moses – "Who appointed you a ruler and a judge?" – is so significant to Stephen that he mentions it twice in his speech before the Sanhedrin (see also Acts 7:35).

Moses clearly dealt with adversity. But even though some of the opposition he faced was due to the Israelites not recognizing God's call upon his life, Moses' own shortcomings were to blame as well – killing the Egyptian certainly didn't help matters! And therefore, Moses' blunders early on blocked an early path to leadership of his people. "Moses fled and became an exile in the land of Midian" (Acts 7:29b).

The Israelites, of course, had manifold issues of their own, displayed in numerous acts of rebellion in the wilderness. Stephen sums up his ancestors' wicked deeds as he describes the account of the golden calf: "Our forefathers were unwilling to obey [Moses], but pushed him away, and in their hearts turned back to Egypt. They told Aaron: Make us gods who will go before us. As for this Moses who brought us out of the land of Egypt, we don't know what's become of him" (Acts 7:39-40).

Aliens Suffer Affliction

Moses' life teaches us that spiritual aliens must be prepared for rejection. When the message we share with others announces that people are sinful and need cleansing, we should not be surprised if we as the messengers are ignored, scorned or attacked. The Lord of all creation came to bring life to the world He created, and men rejected Him. "He came to His own, and His own did not receive Him" (Jn. 1:11, NKJV).

Through all the ups and downs of life and leadership, Moses does, by God's grace, adopt a foreigner mindset for the right reasons: "By faith Moses, when he had grown up, refused to be called the son of Pharaoh's daughter and chose to suffer with the people of God rather than to enjoy the short-lived pleasure of sin. For he considered reproach for the sake of the Messiah to be greater wealth than the treasures of Egypt, since his attention was on the reward. By faith he left Egypt behind, not being afraid of the king's anger, for he persevered, as one who sees Him who is invisible" (Heb. 11:24-27).

Spiritual aliens like Moses need to be ready to have their lives – and comfort – disrupted.

Early in his life, Moses seemed to have every advantage. Stephen informs us – despite the deliverer's own protestations to God about a lack of speaking ability – that "Moses was educated in all the wisdom of the Egyptians, and was powerful in his speech and actions" (Acts 7:22).

But as we've seen, those Moses was supposed to lead dismissed his credentials, and Moses' leadership of his kinspeople was fraught with challenges and frustrations. Old Testament passages tell us that the Israelites "became stiff-necked and appointed a leader to return to their slavery in Egypt" (Neh. 9:17) and "in the camp they were envious of Moses and of Aaron" (Ps. 106:16) and that they "angered the Lord at the waters of Meribah, and Moses suffered because of them" (Ps. 106:32).

Yet what happened to Moses was no aberration. Rejection from others is the prevailing pattern for biblical aliens.

Traveling the Road of Resistance

Consider the life of Joseph in the Old Testament: He achieves comfort in his family of origin, becoming his father's favorite – then gets sold into slavery. He next achieves comfort in his new household, becoming second in command under Potiphar – then gets thrown into prison. He achieves comfort in prison, becoming second in command under the warden – then has his one hope for freedom, the chief cupbearer, forget about him. He finally achieves comfort in the royal palace, becoming second in command under Pharaoh – then has buried tensions with his brothers spring to the surface as those men show up in Egypt for food.

Being a spiritual alien is accepting that the pursuit of God's purposes will create earthly discomfort. "Now those who say such things make it clear that they are seeking a homeland. If they had been remembering that land they came from, they would have had opportunity to return. But they now aspire to a better land – a heavenly one. Therefore, God is not ashamed to be called their God, for He has prepared a city for them" (Heb. 11:14-16).

After a number of years in my first pastorate, I sensed a call of God to gain more experience in evangelism, and to also use a change of scenery to align with a denomination that had a high view of Scripture. I sought to take a major step of faith as we moved to central Ohio, with my heart confident that God would work out all the day-to-day details.

Some of the people we knew were mystified that I was leaving a healthy congregation and walking blind into the unknown – and with that decision, taking my family with me. But I believed that the Lord was calling us to an alien adventure – and was more correct on that count that I knew at the time!

We took classes at a Bible college sponsored by our new denomination. Soon it was time for me to get into the workplace. I had come to feel sure that God had opened a door for me to work in a cabinet shop owned by a member of the church we attended. Now in the back of my mind I knew that handyman and carpentry skills were not really in my repertoire, let alone detailed cabinetry work. However, I signed up and the owner said we'd give it a try for three months.

The work was incredibly challenging for me. I made more than my share of mistakes, yet as we got close to the three-month mark, I thought I was picking up some skills and getting better. Therefore, my boss's pulling me aside at the end of a work week caught me off-guard. And his short statement, "I don't think this is going to work out," turned my world upside down.

The drive home was about 30 minutes, and that was certainly the longest half hour of my life. I walked into our small apartment, where my wife was surrounded by three young children – all four totally dependent on my income for support. I told Kay, "I am sorry that I am a failure." Never did my words line up so well with my thoughts and feelings.

My wife was amazingly gracious, and even more so was our Lord. In hindsight, this experience was invaluable for my growth as a believer – but my preference is to never go through something like that again!

I did learn, to paraphrase the Dutch Christian Corrie ten Boom, whose trials outclassed mine in every way, that no matter how deep the pit I felt I was in, our God is deeper still. I learned that spiritual aliens must accept the reality of rough waves when we get out of the boat and walk with Christ on the water. I learned that sometimes those waters will get the best of us and we'll go under – but Jesus is still there, ready to pull us up.

Discipleship Means Disruption

Have you ever experienced crisis that you ushered into your life because you were genuinely following Jesus? Have you ever delved into uncertainty or anguish because of ministry to a troubled person, or been embarrassed because you attempted to witness to an unbeliever, or was verbally attacked because you stood for a biblical truth? If you answer these questions in the negative, you might do well to ask yourself if you have ever been engaged in the process of discipleship.

> Then Jesus said to His disciples, 'If anyone wants to come with Me, he must deny himself, take up his cross, and follow Me'" (Mt. 16:24). "I assure you: Unless a grain of wheat falls into the ground and dies, it remains by itself. But if it dies, it produces a large crop. The one who loves his life will lose it, and the one who hates his life in this world will keep it for eternal life. If anyone serves Me, he must follow Me" (Jn. 12:24-26a).

Moses, living a millennium and a half before Jesus, nevertheless lived *for Jesus*: "He regarded abuse suffered for Christ to be greater wealth than the treasures of Egypt, for his eyes were fixed on the reward" (Heb. 11:26, NET).

This impulse that we see in Moses shines a spotlight on a huge stumbling block in our day. The pitfall for us is hoping that God will find a place in our world without His priorities diverting us from our own personal goals. In this scenario, we then want something else at the center of who we are – earthly success or financial gain or material comfort – while desiring that the living Lord somehow stay on the periphery.

But discipleship never works that way. You can't orient your life around your own personal pleasure and continue to be a disciple. You can't orient your life around the pursuit of riches and continue to be a disciple. You can't orient your life around fame and notoriety and continue to be a disciple. You can't orient your life even around essentially good things, like family and industry and community, and continue to be a disciple.

In our daily lives, Christ will either be Lord of all, or Lord not at all.

Chapter 8

Ruth and Steadfastness

The resurrected Jesus appeared to some disciples on the road to Emmaus, and we find this statement in the account of that appearance: "Then beginning with Moses and all the Prophets, He interpreted for them the things concerning Himself in all the Scriptures" (Lk. 24:27) In this context some readers might ask, "What do you mean 'things concerning [Christ] in all the Scriptures'? The only Bible available at the time was the Old Testament – how could they see Jesus there?"

As we've discussed already, an important way is through typology. The most common Old Testament types point to Jesus Christ, yet none of those who do typify the Savior, by any means, capture all of whom the Messiah is or all of what He does.

Nevertheless, Old Testament types frequently capture very significant aspects of Christ. For example, Joseph is rejected by his brethren but ends up being his people's redeemer – which can be said of Moses as well – and of course we see this same reality in the life of Jesus.

In this chapter I want to look at the Old Testament character Ruth and how she models an alien lifestyle. But alongside of lessons from this Moabite woman's life, I also want to present

Ruth's mother-in-law – Naomi – as a type of Christ. First, let's delve into the narrative of the book that bears Ruth's name.

Unexpected Challenges

Although the Moabitess Ruth does indeed demonstrate an alien existence, she did not initially volunteer to live the life of a foreigner. However, that is what came her way after her husband, brother-in-law and father-in-law all died prematurely in Moab, following the earlier journey of an Israelite couple (Elimelech and Naomi) coming to her area with their two adult sons during a famine.

The three women who survived the deaths of their three husbands were left with a momentous choice: Stay in Moab or go back to the Bethlehem area. Naomi, the Jewish mother-in-law, made clear her advice to her two Moabite daughters-in-law, Orpah and Ruth: "She said to them, 'Each of you go back to your mother's home. May the Lord show faithful love to you as you have shown to the dead and to me. May the Lord enable each of you to find security in the house of your new husband'" (Ruth 1:8-9a).

Naomi is, in a particular and narrow way, a type of Christ. But wait a minute, a Bible student might say in response, "Isn't the obvious type of Christ in this Old Testament book Boaz, the kinsman-redeemer?" Yes, that is true, and later in the book of Ruth we find him entering the story to represent the blessings and rewards of the Savior, showered on Ruth to conclude this entire account. This Gentile woman eventually finds "security in the house of [her] new husband" (Ruth 1:9), which can be paralleled with the believer finding spiritual security in the Father's house (Jn. 14:2) through the agency of the Bridegroom Jesus Christ.

But while Boaz represents abundance found in Christ, Naomi represents the cost and travail that the Lord ordains for us, and the sequence of Ruth first showing loyalty to Naomi before experiencing, secondly, the abundance of Boaz, is by no means coincidental. Cost comes before comfort. Crucifixion always comes before Resurrection. Suffering always comes before glory.

Heartbroken by the loss of the dearest men in her life, not to mention the loss of her livelihood, Naomi instructs others not to call her by her given name, which means "pleasant," but rather Mara, which means "bitter." In this way she represents the One we call the Suffering Servant, who is described with these words: "He was despised and rejected by men, a man of suffering who knew what sickness was. He was like one people turned away from; He was despised, and we didn't value Him" (Isa. 53:3).

Naomi says that "the Lord's hand has turned against" her and that "the Almighty has afflicted" her (Ruth 1:13, 21) and Isaiah says the Suffering Servant was "struck down by God, and afflicted" and that "the Lord has punished Him" (Isa. 53:4, 6). Naomi loses all the men closest to her, and the same held true for Jesus – one disciple betrayed Him, one denied Him, and the others forsook Him.

But despite the travail experienced by both type (Naomi) and Fulfillment (Christ), both saw the fruit of their personal labors. After just describing the anguish of the Suffering Servant, Isaiah continues on to proclaim, "He will see His [spiritual] seed, He will prolong His days" (Isa. 53:10) while in the book of Ruth we read that "Naomi took [the son born to Ruth and Boaz], placed him on her lap, and took care of him. The neighbor women said, 'A son has been born to Naomi,' and they named him Obed" (Ruth 4:16-17a).

There are additional similarities between Naomi and Christ. Just as Naomi warns both Orpah and Ruth of a price to pay in following their mother-in-law, so does the Lord of glory when it comes to men and women claiming allegiance to Him:

> No one who puts his hand to the plow and looks back is fit for the kingdom of God" (Lk. 9:62). "If anyone comes to Me and does not hate his own father and mother, wife and children, brothers and sisters – yes, and even his own life – he cannot be

My disciple. Whoever does not bear his own cross and come after Me cannot be My disciple" (Lk. 14:26-27).

Note that early in the book of Ruth, we have Naomi's two daughters-in-law needing to make fateful decisions – and it turns out that we're given a powerful contrast in this account. Let me pause for a moment here and mention that this literary feature of contrast plays prominently in biblical storytelling from the beginning. Cain's unacceptable approach to God is contrasted to his brother Abel's acceptable approach to God in Genesis 4. Judah's unsuccessful handling of sexual temptation, in Genesis 38, is contrasted with his brother Joseph's successful handling of sexual temptation in Genesis 39.

And Paul lays out with surgical precision the contrast between the first Adam and the last Adam: "Since by the one man's trespass, death reigned through that one man, how much more will those who receive the overflow of grace and the gift of righteousness reign in life through the one man, Jesus Christ. So then, as through one trespass there is condemnation for everyone, so also through one righteous act there is life-giving justification for everyone. For just as through one man's disobedience the many were made sinners, so also through the one man's obedience the many will be made righteous" (Rom. 5:17-19).

A Difficult Decision

Now let's come back to the contrast between Orpah and Ruth presented early in the Old Testament book that bears Ruth's name.

[Naomi] said to them, 'Each of you go back to your mother's home. May the Lord show faithful love to you as you have shown to the dead and to me. May the Lord enable each of you to find security in the house of your new husband.' She kissed them, and they wept loudly. 'No,' they said to her. 'We will go with you to your people.' But Naomi replied, 'Return home, my daughters. Why do you want to go with me? Am I able to have any more sons who could become your husbands? Return home, my daughters. Go on, for I am too old to have another husband. Even if I thought there was still hope for me to have a husband tonight and to bear sons, would you be willing to wait for them to grow up? Would you restrain yourselves from remarrying? No, my daughters, my life is much too bitter for you to share, because the Lord's hand has turned against me.' Again they wept loudly, and Orpah kissed her mother-in-law, but Ruth clung to her" (Ruth 1:8-14).

When Naomi warns her daughters-in-law, as described above, we at first see no difference between the two younger women, with weeping all around. As the mother-in-law speaks her peace, the younger women feel the older woman's heartbreak. But then the moment of truth comes. Orpah, representing the casual believer, politely kisses the type of Christ; Ruth, however, representing the committed disciple, passionately *clutches* the type of Christ.

Some scholars say that the Hebrew word *Orpah* is from a noun meaning "back of the neck" and related to a verb meaning "to turn one's back," which describes Orpah's eventual response to Naomi. And scholars say that the Hebrew word *Ruth* is from the noun "friendship," taken from the word "friend," which describes Ruth's response to Naomi.

Orpah will show respect to her mother-in-law, but she will go her own way. Ruth, on the other hand, will respond in a manner very similar to the genuine Christian who hears, and heeds, the words of Jesus explaining the cost. That is to say, Ruth will commit herself unreservedly: "Do not persuade me to leave you or go back and not follow you. For wherever you go, I will go, and wherever you live, I will live; your people will be my people, and your God will be my God" (Ruth 1:16).

Relevance for Today

The symbolism found in the book of Ruth is incredibly relevant for so much of the modern world. In the United States, despite its weighty Christian influence and legacy, surveys show disconcerting if not appalling results. Pollsters found that among one group of those claiming Christ:

> More than half (58 percent) believe that God accepts the worship of all religions, including Christianity, Judaism, and Islam. More than half (56 percent) agree that worshiping alone or with one's family is a valid replacement for regularly attending church. More than half (55 percent) believe the Holy Spirit is a force but is not a personal being. More than half (55 percent) agree that 'everyone sins a little, but most people are good by nature.'"[1]

And these results were not gathered from liberal denominations – these results were attributed to those the pollsters consider evangelicals, that is to say, those defined as described below:

"The survey categorized people as having evangelical beliefs if they strongly agreed with the following four statements:

The Bible is the highest authority for what I believe. It is very important for me personally to encourage non-Christians to trust Jesus Christ as their Savior. Jesus Christ's death on the cross is the only sacrifice that could remove the penalty of my sin. Only those who trust in Jesus Christ alone as their Savior receive God's free gift of eternal salvation."[2]

---

1. https://www.thegospelcoalition.org/article/state-theology-2022/, accessed March 2023.
2. https://www.thegospelcoalition.org/article/state-theology-2022/, accessed March 2023.

THIS RESEARCH IS A REMINDER THAT MEN AND WOMEN aligning themselves with a ringing commitment to Scripture as authoritative and to Jesus as Redeemer can be incredibly misguided when it comes to fundamental theological beliefs and practices. It has been said for decades that the church in America is a mile wide and an inch deep.

A friend of mine mentioned that she and her husband stopped attending a multi-campus church, considered to be one of the most evangelical congregations in its county, when, before the Sunday service, recorded secular music was played featuring a popular singer known for her immoral lifestyle and lyrics. We're surrounded by both individuals and groupings of nominal faith.

Matching Works to One's Words

On the other hand, I have a ministry friend who has been serving Christ for decades in rural Mexico. In the shadow of drug gangs, he has dug water wells that have been incredible blessings for local communities and he and his wife have run an orphanage for needy youngsters. He interprets the New Testament as simply and literally as possible, and his family's theme verse has been: "Pure and undefiled religion before our God and Father is this: to look after orphans and widows in their distress and to keep oneself unstained by the world" (Jas. 1:27).

This couple and their eleven children have cared for a wide variety of kids over the years, those without ready parenting available to them and often those with severe disabilities, many of them very difficult to train and teach and discipline. Theirs is a full-time ministry, and to my knowledge they've never made any direct appeal for funding. Once they were on a ministry furlough and stayed with us, and he was scheduled to speak at an evening meeting for the church I was pastoring. I asked him ahead of time if we could receive an offering for his ministry. He looked at me and said, "I'd rather you didn't," and to this day I'm not sure why he didn't want an offering when it was made available, and I may never find out, which I'm completely comfortable with. I didn't push him at the time to discover why because it felt to me like I was in some way approaching holy ground.

This is an individual who runs from publicity when other Christians run toward it, who will go out of his way to make things right when he is the only person who believes he may have erred. This is the kind of friend where, if I said I had an hour's worth of complaints about his behavior (which I certainly do not), he'd listen to me for two. If I went on a long trip and left him with $1,000 of my money for safekeeping, I'd come back and probably have $1,100. As I've said before, I'll say again – I can't know anyone else's heart as God does – but by all accounts, it would seem that this man represents, day in and day out, what Christ looks for in discipleship.

Getting the Order Correct

The Lord has a school of training to make us more like Jesus – the school of suffering. We Christians, especially in the modern West, recoil at the idea of growth through difficulty and hardship, but this theme is shouted at us all through Scripture. We return now to the idea mentioned earlier: Suffering always precedes glory – and suffering, responded to in the right way, God's way, prepares us for glory. Suffering, if responded to in Christlike fashion, scrapes pride and selfishness off of our souls and leaves purity.

Paul says that "we suffer with Him so that we may also be glorified with Him" (Rom. 8:17b) and Peter says that as we "share in the sufferings of the Messiah rejoice, so that you may also rejoice with great joy at the revelation of His glory" (1 Pet. 4:13). "For our momentary light affliction is producing for us an absolutely incomparable eternal weight of glory" (2 Cor. 4:17). "For this I suffer, to the point of being bound like a criminal; but God's message is not bound. This is why I endure all things for the elect: so that they also may obtain salvation, which is in Christ Jesus, with eternal glory. This saying is trustworthy: For if we have died with Him, we will also live with Him; if we endure, we will also reign with Him" (2 Tim. 2:9-12a).

Be suspicious of any path that offers glory without difficulty and discipline. Remember that the devil offered to Jesus such a path: "So he took Him up and showed Him all the kingdoms of the world in a moment of time. The Devil said to Him, 'I will give You their splendor and all this authority, because it has been given over to me, and I can give it to anyone I want. If You, then, will worship me, all will be Yours.' And Jesus answered him, 'It is written: Worship the Lord your God, and serve Him only'" (Lk. 4:5-8).

God brings crucifixion before resurrection. The Lord brings humiliation before exaltation. "God resists the proud, but gives grace to the humble. Humble yourselves therefore under the mighty hand of God, so that He may exalt you in due time" (1 Pet. 5:5c-6). "[Christ] humbled Himself by becoming obedient to the point of death – even to death on a cross. For this reason, God also highly exalted Him and gave Him the name that is above every name" (Phil. 2:8-9).

Ruth is honored by her kinsman-redeemer because she is a spiritual alien: "Boaz answered her, 'Everything you have done for your mother-in-law since your husband's death has been fully reported to me: how you left your father and mother, and the land of your birth, and how you came to a people you didn't previously know. May the Lord reward you for what you have done, and may you receive a full reward from the Lord God of Israel, under whose wings you have come for refuge'" (Ruth 2:11-12).

Faithfulness is Not Forgotten

To be realistic, we must also realize that suffering and sacrificing for Christ can open up avenues leading to personal despair and disillusionment. Sometimes as we go about our alien obedience and servanthood to God, we wonder if He takes any notice of all that we've given up.

In one of my pastorates, I remember a woman checking with me about curriculum for teaching children. This woman had a master's degree in nursing, was doing another master's in theology, and was just about old enough to be my mother. It took some time to realize it, but she was wanting my approval of the curriculum, which came as a shock when that finally dawned on me! And it seems that deeper down, this precious believer wanted to know that her sacrifices had not gone unnoticed – something we can probably all relate to.

When we're serving in the trenches, we do well at times to receive – as from God – those words of the kinsman-redeemer Boaz's: "Everything you have done ... has been fully reported to me: how you left your father and mother, ... and how you came to a people you didn't previously know. May the Lord reward you for what you have done, and may you receive a full reward" (Ruth 2:11-12b).

The Parable of the Talents gives us a window into the gracious response of a Savior who loves to commend: "His master said to him, 'Well done, good and faithful slave! You were faithful over a few things; I will put you in charge of many things. Share your master's joy!'" (Mt. 25:21).

No kingdom effort, done by a spiritual alien in the name of Jesus, will go unnoticed: "If anyone serves Me, the Father will honor him" (Jn. 12:26c). Sometimes we wonder if God sees our sincere attempts to glorify Him and promote His ways. He does! Every time. Rest assured that the Lord does not forget your service and ministry, as insignificant as they may sometimes seem, as you sincerely bless others in the goodness and godliness of the gospel.

Chapter 9

Uriah and Loyalty

The most sensationally scandalous story in all the Bible is that of David and Bathsheba. It's the account of an affair between a usually godly king and a beautiful woman, supplemented by elements of intrigue, betrayal and murder.

The general account: David is on the roof of his palace when he spots Bathsheba bathing. He finds out who this woman is and has her brought to him for a rendezvous. Bathsheba becomes pregnant. Her husband Uriah is a soldier under the king's command, and David orders him back home in hopes that he will lie with his wife and the pregnancy will be glossed over. However, Uriah remembers the deprivations his fellow soldiers are enduring and remains true to his military calling, never sleeping in his own home during his return.

Feeling forced to adopt an alternative plan, David sends Uriah back to the front with, as it were, a sealed death warrant. Outside a city that Israel has under siege, the Israelite commander receives instructions to leave Uriah intentionally unprotected, which he does, with the result that the loyal warrior is slain by enemy soldiers.

The writer of 2 Samuel ends chapter 11 with these words:

"When Uriah's wife heard that her husband Uriah had died, she mourned for him. When the time of mourning ended, David had her brought to his house. She became his wife and bore him a son. However, the Lord considered what David had done to be evil" (2 Sam. 11:26-27).

Going Deeper in the Story

One of the questions Bible readers have asked is, "Did Uriah realize what David was up to?" To answer that question, put yourself in Uriah's sandals. The king calls you alone, one of his elite officers, back from the site of battle to wine and dine you in the palace for no good reason and then encourages you, with a gift, to spend a night at home. And when the king finds out the next day you didn't enter your house, he poses these questions to you: "Haven't you just come from a journey? Why didn't you go home?" (2 Sam. 11:10). And David gets you drunk that second evening and sends you along with the same hope of you sleeping with your wife.

I find it difficult to believe that Uriah, in this set of circumstances, could have been so clueless that he failed to grasp what was happening. When the king from his palace has a direct line of sight to your property and beautiful wife, and singles you out by pulling you from the midst of the battle, and sends you off to your wife after he's had you at his table, and then asks you the next day why you didn't go inside your house – what more would Uriah need to put things together?

Let's further delve into this biblical account. Scriptural passages often contain insights that may not be initially noticed. I'd like to lay out some thoughts from this narrative, going back to when David first discovers that Uriah spends the night at the door of the king's palace instead of staying with Bathsheba:

David questioned Uriah, 'Haven't you just come from a journey? Why didn't you go home?' Uriah answered David, 'The

ark, Israel, and Judah are dwelling in tents, and my master Joab
and his soldiers are camping in the open field. How can I enter
my house to eat and drink and sleep with my wife? As surely as
you live and by your life, I will not do this!'" (2 Sam. 11:10b-11).

Notice Uriah's initial statement to his king when David asks
why he didn't go to his own home: "The ark, Israel, and Judah are
dwelling in tents." The first thing Uriah mentions is the ark of
God, and he states that it is dwelling in a tent.

What is intriguing about Uriah's statement, "The ark ... [is]
dwelling in tents," is that in this same book of 2 Samuel, another
individual, earlier in the narrative, also states that the ark is
dwelling in a tent. And that individual is none other than David
himself:

When the king had settled into his palace and the Lord had
given him rest on every side from all his enemies, the king said to
Nathan the prophet, 'Look, I am living in a cedar house while
the ark of God sits inside tent curtains'" (2 Sam. 7:1-2).

An Alien Outlook

Why is all of this important? Because while David is offended
that the ark is in a tent, Uriah, with that same piece of information, is motivated – he's challenged to go where God sends him.
While David looks to entrench the ark, Uriah looks to emulate
the ark. David loves the ark at rest. Uriah loves the ark on the
move. David loves the ark guarded. Uriah loves the ark unleashed
and released.

When Uriah told David, "The ark ... [is] dwelling in tents," he
was in effect saying to his king, "I will be like the ark – away from
my established home. I will be alien."

Undoubtedly, neither Uriah nor even David understood all
the mysteries of the ark, which, as we've seen, is a type of the
Messiah, Jesus Christ. But I'm confident that both David and

Uriah understood this: The ark represented the presence of the God of Israel.

Back when God commanded Moses to have the ark made, He said: "I will meet with you there above the mercy seat, between the two cherubim that are over the ark of the testimony; I will speak with you from there about all that I command you regarding the Israelites" (Ex. 25:22).

The ark was the central object of the tabernacle and temple, and was never to be taken trivially: "The Lord said to Moses: 'Tell your brother Aaron that he may not come whenever he wants into the holy place behind the veil in front of the mercy seat on the ark or else he will die, because I appear in the cloud above the mercy seat" (Lev. 16:2). Men who treated the ark of the covenant flippantly paid the price with their own lives, as we've seen in some detail in Chapter 5 of this book.

A Mandate to Be on the Move

Thus, we have two accounts in 2 Samuel of someone saying the ark is in a tent: David when he wants to build a temple, and Uriah when he gives an account to his king. But the parallels don't end there.

Note that 2 Samuel 7, the account of David being unhappy with the ark in a tent, begins with the words, "When the king had settled into his palace." And 2 Samuel 11, the account of David's affair with Bathsheba, in which Uriah states that he will dwell apart from any sturdy building as the ark does, begins with these words:

> In the spring when kings march out to war, David sent Joab with his officers and all Israel. They destroyed the Ammonites and besieged Rabbah [the capital city of the Ammonites], but David remained in Jerusalem" (v. 1).

Both accounts speak of David planting himself firmly in his

capital. That is to say, David, at least in these instances, was rejecting an alien role.

Note the setting in which David asked that the ark of the covenant be placed in a permanent house. He had settled comfortably into his palace, having set his enemies back on their heels. David, in a position that was static, was ready to maintain his comfort and convenience and stop pursuing the things of God.

God then responds to David, "When have I asked my people to build a house for my name?"

Permission is Not Preference

Now, at the same time, God does go along with the overall "plan" – David's plan to see a temple erected – in many respects. However, that doesn't mean that men's plans are God's initiative and delight. In fact, the kingship, which David was called to, is a prime example of this principle. Having a king over Israel wasn't God's idea, but man's! Yet God was gracious enough to go along with it, as abnormal as that approach may seem.

David had lived many years conquering any obstacle for the sake of God Almighty. It was David who slaughtered Goliath, it was David who suffered under Saul, and it was David who sang the praises of God for Israel. In all the history of national Israel, dominant force in the Promised Land, it was David's reign which hit the high mark of a golden age, and the coming Messiah was identified as a Son *of David*.

But in 2 Samuel 11, we have David, man after God's own heart, breaking every major commandment in the Book while Uriah, a Hittite – a Gentile foreigner – is consistently demonstrating integrity and character through waves of deception and betrayal, all the way up to his own assassination. Let that sink in. The spiritual aliens among us are not always the ones we would have predicted.

Previously David was hunted by a king (Saul) who was afraid

of something (the kingship) taken away from him. Now David was the hunter and king who was afraid he couldn't take something (sexual privilege) away from someone else and keep it hidden from public view.

David, who wouldn't drink a drop of water his elite guard risked their lives for, who wouldn't accept without payment the threshing floor of Araunah the Jebusite[1], now, in a season of spiritual weakness, utterly destroys the life of one of his most loyal servants for the sake of not being embarrassed.

When David stopped being an alien, as clearly revealed in his summoning Bathsheba, he dove headlong into serious trouble and heartache for himself and others.

The Call to Continue

David settled. That is to say, the David on the warpath gave way to a David hanging back from the battle. David pursuing God's enemies in the land gave way to David pursuing a pretty woman next door. The king of Israel was no longer an alien invading enemy territory, but becoming more and more comfortable with convenience and ease, even to the point of betraying and murdering perhaps the most loyal soldier he would ever have – a warrior who would carry his own death sentence back to the battlefield, no doubt with a very educated guess as to the information in the palm of his own hand.

It wasn't wrong of David to desire a permanent spiritual rest from all conflict. What was wrong was his design to attempt to have that kind of rest *in this life*. That kind of "eternal settledness" only arrives for us in the next life.

And we'd be fools to ignore the warning that exists here for us.

I've been a fan of basketball as long as I can remember. I played in high school, and I've coached in various youth leagues.

---

1. For these two accounts, see 2 Sam. 23:13-17 and 2 Sam. 24:1-25, respectively.

In the NBA, they talk about someone "settling." That is, on a certain night, a player on offense will catch a pass 18 or 20 feet from the basket. To then dribble the ball and drive toward the goal means exerting tremendous energy only to meet the force of the opposition. It means to often get whacked by some very strong athletes, defenders who are also so quick the referee may or may not call a foul. And the offensive player – the guy who is tempted to "settle" – may have flown in on a red-eye flight to reach the city where the game is taking place. Who can blame the player for just hoisting up 19-foot shots, even if they're not part of the team's strategy?

It's easy for Christians to settle. And it's easy for those who settle to label genuine discipleship "extremism" or "zeal without knowledge." It's easy to call new ventures at an advanced age "a lack of discernment."

And it's easy to lounge on the roof of your palace when you should be fighting a war.

It's convenient to relax and settle into a culture and then begin to empathize with its messages. It's easy to end up excusing disobedience around us. "Well, he did get revenge, but they had it coming to them," or, "Well, she did commit adultery, but look at the bad hand she was dealt," or, "Well, they're in a homosexual relationship, but they've got to have their needs met." And then before long we're excusing our own personal path away from biblical ethics as well.

This account in 2 Samuel is a lesson in backsliding, in lethargy, in settling down and letting the call of God and the demands of His kingdom flow on down the river. Jesus still says to us, "If anyone wants to come with Me, he must deny himself, take up his cross daily, and follow Me" (Lk. 9:23b).

Keeping It Current

Notice that little word "daily." Maybe you repented of your sins and put your trust in Christ 10, 20 or 40 years ago. That's truly wonderful; praise God for that starting point. But how are you following Him today? Are you spending time in the Scriptures and prayer in order to have the Lord's perspective on life and to be conformed to the image of Christ? What is taking place in your life currently that demonstrates discipleship, that puts on display your yielding of preferences and you giving up what you want for what Jesus wants?

As we see in 2 Samuel 11, David the warrior quit fighting. For the mature believer today, a primary arena for continuing to fight instead of deciding to settle is the arena of seeking to lead others to Christ. In modern Western society, this tends to be time-consuming. Unbelievers are distracted by the wealth and comforts of our age and confused by the ideologies of false philosophies. It takes energy to witness, and to relate, and to demonstrate the way of Jesus.

As I mentioned in an earlier chapter, at one point my family and I lived on the west side of Columbus, Ohio, in order to build relationships with non-Christians. Across the yard lived two gay men in a small apartment, and my family occupied a similar residence. I sought to get to know those men and communicate something of the biblical Christ to them.

One of them, whom I'll call Walter, became HIV-positive. That is to say, he had a life-threatening condition. I visited him in the hospital, where at the time he had a tube going down his throat and couldn't speak. I went over the fundamentals of the gospel and asked him if he wanted to surrender his life to Christ.

Walter nodded. I said, "You realize that you have to turn your back on your old way of life?" Walter nodded again, and I led him in prayer to repent of his sins and enter into a relationship with Christ.

The next time I came back to the hospital, I was met in the hallway by Walter's roommate, Larry, who was a reserved and withdrawing type. Larry did not for a moment appreciate Walter's recent decision to commit himself to Christ, and so he brought along a friend who was much more vocal and confrontational than he was.

I remember a short, heated discussion in that hallway in which the friend got in my face with how he thought I was in the wrong, to which I said, "Look, it's Walter's decision to make, not anybody else's."

Those words turned out to be prophetic, but not in the way I had hoped. Walter regained his health, was dismissed from the hospital, and went back to live with Larry and the ungodly life-style that they had earlier engaged in.

Tough Times Will Come

God's followers will suffer setbacks. In my case, my counsel was left to perish. In Uriah's case, *his life* was left to perish. But our focus is on faithfulness to the Lord's agenda, regardless of how others respond to our message. Paul was committed to proclaiming Christ "through glory and dishonor, through slander and good report" (2 Cor. 6:8a).

Whatever the outcome, though, what greater glory can ascend to God than when we lay down our preferences and our comforts and our personal desires in order to call people toward and into the kingdom of heaven?

But all the while we need to remember this strange truth: While we earnestly seek genuine spiritual response, kingdom success can actually pose a certain danger for the Christian! The relief and reward that come from mastering a certain skill or having a ministry blossom can set the stage for spiritual stagnation and relying on one's experience and expertise instead of crying out to God for new breakthroughs from heaven. Just look at David the conqueror staying home from war and sinning with Bathsheba or, earlier in the Old Testament, at Gideon steering his family and nation toward idolatry after incredible military victories.

The call, however, is to find our "settledness" and stability in the peace and promises of God, regardless of the challenges, and successes, He allows us to experience in this life.

Many Christians, though, have created a cheap imitation of this. The temptation for us is to try to find our "settledness" and stability in earthly materialism, while looking for adventure in some hobby or business pursuit, or the expense of some vacation or possession. In other words, we end up pursuing earthly treasures instead of accumulating spiritual ones. And since we're not trying to find tranquility or adventure in drugs or sex, we think we're in great shape spiritually.

Giving the Glory to God

It's telling that at the very end of his earthly existence, David does not recollect his military conquests or his kingly reign. Instead, he remembers the Almighty bringing deliverance to him. What is mentioned toward the end of life is not the soldier's strength, but God's power in light of the king's weakness: "David [originally] spoke the words of this song to the Lord on the day the Lord rescued him from the hand of all his enemies and from the hand of Saul" (2 Sam. 22:1).

David regains an alien attitude: "I called to the Lord, who is worthy of praise, and I was saved from my enemies. For the waves of death engulfed me; the torrents of destruction terrified me. The ropes of Sheol entangled me; the snares of death confronted me. I called to the Lord in my distress; I called to my God. From His temple He heard my voice, and my cry for help reached His ears" (2 Sam. 22:4-7). David came back to his former approach, as voiced in the Psalms: "Hear my prayer, Lord, and listen to my cry for help; do not be silent at my tears. For I am a foreigner residing with You, a sojourner like all my fathers" (39:12).

God repeatedly carries out a tightrope walk with His people. He desires to pour out blessing and comfort and even prosperity upon us, but to do so almost invariably causes us to know lethargy and distance created between Him and us. He knows that affliction is the schoolhouse in which we learn. God is delighted to bring Israel into Canaan, in that He gives His people peace and a measure of security, but God is loath to see His people lapse into religious comfort as David did.

Chapter 10

Attributes of an Alien

We're called to be spiritual aliens, owing allegiance to a kingdom different than the one we're currently living in. We're to be existing "in the world" but "not of the world." While our loyalty to Christ reveals itself in many ways, Scripture directly connects several particular attributes with an alien approach:

- Love Over Revenge
- Simplicity Over Luxury
- Faith Over Fear

Let's analyze how Jesus and His apostles teach us these principles and instruct us how to live them out in practical ways.

Love Over Revenge

A Christian woman, known for speaking to church ladies' groups, was asked to address a women's gathering in a congregation she was not acquainted with. And the topic was already selected: How to stock up and prepare for an anticipated downturn, or even chaos, in society.

The speaker began to beg off politely: "We Christians could stockpile for our own benefit, but there would still be neighbors coming to our doors in need of food and other supplies." However, the church representative had a ready reply for the speaker: "That's why we have guns and ammunition."

For those of us who claim to follow Jesus of Nazareth, if our approach is to rely on guns and ammunition then the true battle – a spiritual battle – is already lost. "'My kingdom is not of this world,' said Jesus. 'If My kingdom were of this world, My servants would fight, so that I wouldn't be handed over to the Jews. As it is, My kingdom does not have its origin here'" (Jn. 18:36). Jesus taught, and lived out, an alien approach when it comes to practically loving those opposed to us.

Many claiming to walk with Christ seem to have never contemplated these alien marching orders from the Master: "You have heard that it was said, An eye for an eye and a tooth for a tooth. But I tell you, don't resist an evildoer. On the contrary, if anyone slaps you on your right cheek, turn the other to him also. As for the one who wants to sue you and take away your shirt, let him have your coat as well. And if anyone forces you to go one mile, go with him two. Give to the one who asks you, and don't turn away from the one who wants to borrow from you. You have heard that it was said, Love your neighbor and hate your enemy. But I tell you, love your enemies and pray for those who persecute you, so that you may be sons of your Father in heaven" (Mt. 5:38-45a).

Jesus repeatedly taught the opposite of human reasoning. We say, "Be sure to fight for your rights." Christ says, "Be sure to show sacrificial love to others." We say, "Be sure to demand much from others." Christ says, "Be sure to demand much from yourself." We say, "Be sure to have enough for yourself." Christ says, "Be sure to give enough to others." We say, "Be sure to have the upper hand." Christ says, "Be sure to bless your enemies.'

We sometimes misconstrue the words of Jesus. He never said, "You need to love yourself before you can love others," but that's what we often teach as churches. Christ's actual instruction (repeating a verse from Leviticus) is: Love others the way you already love yourself. And Paul agrees with this principle that we already love ourselves: "For no one ever hates his own flesh, but provides and cares for it" (Eph. 5:29a).

Christ taught repeatedly a willingness to suffer in order to return good for evil. And He practiced precisely what He preached. This was Someone who could have called roughly 70,000 angels to deliver Himself from arrest by the authorities. This was Someone who could wreak justifiable havoc on His enemies, but from the cross prayed: "Father, forgive them, because they do not know what they are doing" (Lk. 23:34).

Jesus experienced one of the most torturous deaths possible as He hung between two criminals; but He was not only guiltless in court, He was also innocent of any sin.

IN THE NETHERLANDS IN 1569, A CHRISTIAN NAMED Dirk Willems was imprisoned for his commitment to the Lord and to the Scriptures. He made a way of escape out of a window using knotted rags as a ladder. A pond, frozen on the surface, lay close to the prison, and as Dirk made his way across, a deputy came charging after him. Dirk, having lost weight due to the smaller food portions that prisoners received, made his way over the ice, but the heavier deputy was not so fortunate.

When the deputy fell through the surface, his life in danger, Dirk could've celebrated the Lord's "deliverance," but he knew that Christ taught him to love his enemies. There was only one thing to do, and Dirk returned to the pond and pulled the deputy out. He was then re-apprehended, placed into a more secure cell, and shortly thereafter met a martyr's death in flames at the stake.

Willems' account brings to mind these words: "Some men were tortured, not accepting release, so that they might gain a better resurrection, and others experienced mockings and scourgings, as well as bonds and imprisonment. They were stoned, they were sawed in two, they died by the sword, they wandered about in sheepskins, in goatskins, destitute, afflicted, and mistreated. The world was not worthy of them" (Heb. 11:35b-38).

We're not called to be settlers; we're called to be aliens. We're not called to theorize about discipleship from a safe distance, we're called to follow Jesus in daily living. We're not called to simply observe the Scriptures, but to obey the Scriptures. We're not here to live for ourselves, but to live for Christ and others.

Simplicity Over Luxury

> And I say this, brothers: the time is limited, so from now on ... those who buy [should be] as though they did not possess, and those who use the world as though they did not make full use of it. For this world in its current form is passing away" (1 Cor. 7:29a, 30c-31).

When it comes to financial stewardship, as with so many aspects of life, this world is not our home. We should purchase, or not purchase, services and goods as though this current existence is passing away – because it surely is, no matter how stable it seems in the moment.

The man or woman who has been delivered from this world's impulses and passions will be free to pour resources into what really matters. As Christ transforms us into His disciples, the shiny goods and services calling for our money and attention are seen for the emptiness they often represent, and our priority will be on the kingdom of God.

> Don't collect for yourselves treasures on earth, where moth and rust destroy and where thieves break in and steal. But collect for yourselves treasures in heaven, where neither moth nor rust

destroys, and where thieves don't break in and steal. For where your treasure is, there your heart will be also" (Mt. 6:19-21).

Note that very last sentence. We tend to say, "Well, I may have a lot of luxurious possessions and assets, but my heart is in the right place." Jesus teaches us: No, actually, it works just the opposite way.

The decisions we make with our money – for example, buying nicer and nicer things for ourselves instead of contributing to kingdom values and causes – guide our hearts. Our hearts will then follow our financial decisions and when we seek luxury, our hearts become colder for Christ and more focused on earthly things. "You cannot serve God and money" (Mt. 6:24b, ESV).

The apostle James rebukes Christians for "liv[ing] luxuriously on the land and hav[ing] indulged" themselves (Jas. 5:5a), just as Christ condemned the religious leaders for being "full of greed and self-indulgence" (Mt. 23:25c). Paul warns that the widow "who is self-indulgent is dead even while she lives" (1 Tim. 5:6).

We need to think biblically about how much we spend on cars and clothing. We need to be stewards when it comes to how high a standard of comfort and convenience we maintain. A bloated lifestyle is so easy to slide into. Although we like to ignore this truth, money spent on luxuries and niceties is money not spent on advancing the kingdom of God. As followers of Christ, we are not to be controlled by marketing and sales pitches, but by the Spirit of the living God.

Now to be clear, when I speak of simplicity, I don't mean always buying the least expensive item. An experienced craftsman knows that if he buys cheap tools, he's just going to spend more resources in the long run with faulty work and broken equipment. And establishing the same principle from another angle, I've had friends who kept a spacious home, but it served as a Christ-centered refuge to a multitude of folks on countless occasions.

Stewardship and Statistics

But here's a statistic to put things in perspective: Did you know that a staggering one of every nine persons across the globe is supported by funds sent home by migrant workers? At the time of this writing, that comes to about 900 million people. These remittances make up three times the amount of international aid – official development assistance and foreign direct investment – combined.

And those migrant workers are sending back home 15 percent of what they earn.[1] Think about that. These workers are aliens in places of opportunity, and they conceivably could cut their ties to clan and tribe and just keep everything for themselves. But they have an allegiance to a cause, a "kingdom" if you will, typically of flesh-and-blood relation.

So, migrant workers send back home 15% of their income, while American Christians, typically much wealthier than these migrant workers, on average give – are you ready for how low this number is? – 2.5% of our income.

It's possible to rationalize that percentage of giving with thoughts like, *well, we have to pay off our college debt or house, or, we have to raise our kids, or, aren't we allowed to enjoy life?* But do you know what the percentage of giving for American Christians was during the Great Depression?

3.3%.[2]

Who are the true aliens here – Christians in the U.S., or migrant workers around the world? Who is less tied to their material resources? Who is more greatly experiencing the blessing of generous giving?

And note this account from the life of Jesus: "Sitting across from the temple treasury, He watched how the crowd dropped

1. https://news.un.org/en/story/2019/06/1040581, accessed August 2023.
2. https://www.christianitytoday.com/ct/2020/august-web-only/most-gener ous-not-who-you-expect-vertical-generosity.html, accessed August 2023.

money into the treasury. Many rich people were putting in large sums. And a poor widow came and dropped in two tiny coins worth very little. Summoning His disciples, He said to them, 'I assure you: This poor widow has put in more than all those giving to the temple treasury. For they all gave out of their surplus, but she out of her poverty has put in everything she possessed – all she had to live on'" (Mk. 12:41-44).

Christ has no problem whatsoever sitting down where the money is given and watching to see what each person gives! And this may be news for some people – He's still watching today.

Faith Over Fear

Many people have the idea that before Christ came, followers of God had to stack up good deeds and earn their way into a saving relationship with Him. But this has always been impossible. Since the Fall, God's people have approached Him, fellowshipped with Him and served Him through faith. The writer of Hebrews makes this abundantly clear:

By faith, Enoch was taken away so that he did not experience death, and he was not to be found because God took him away. For prior to his transformation he was approved, having pleased God. Now without faith it is impossible to please God, for the one who draws near to Him must believe that He exists and rewards those who seek Him. By faith Noah, after being warned about what was not yet seen, in reverence built an ark to deliver his family. By this he condemned the world and became an heir of the righteousness that comes by faith. By faith Abraham, when he was called, obeyed and went out to a place he was going to receive as an inheritance; he went out, not knowing where he was going. By faith he stayed as a foreigner in the land of promise, living in tents with Isaac and Jacob, co-heirs of the same promise. For he was looking forward to the city that has foundations, whose architect and builder is God" (Heb. 11:5-10).

Each of the believers mentioned in the passage above was a pioneer. That is to say, each one blazed a trail into new spiritual territory. And each man sacrificed something significant to travel that uncharted domain as he pursued the purposes of God.

Let's look first of all at Enoch. While others coming before and after this patriarch simply lived – simply existed – this man walked with God. Enoch could have succumbed to the fear of being different, but in faith he sacrificed his time – one of our most precious commodities – to experience a truly deep intimacy with the Lord.

While others capitulated to selfishness and violence, Noah preached righteousness and prepared for judgment. Noah could have feared putting all his eggs in the solitary basket of God's instructions, but in faith he sacrificed his reputation – taking years to build a massive ark because of obedience to his Lord and devotion to his family.

While others settled into accustomed routines and took advantage of homegrown opportunities, Abraham rose and left, destination unknown – but Provider known well. Abraham could have feared leaving everything that was familiar, but in faith sacrificed the comforts of hearth and home – walking a lonely pathway as he waited for the promises of God to materialize.

Abraham is a type of the spiritual alien on mission to impact others for God's purposes. As a geographical and spiritual foreigner, he experienced both the blessings and the burdens that come with stepping out into the mysterious domain where the Lord walks ahead of His followers.

Desperation and Dependency

An alien leaves the familiar and the comfortable in order to demonstrate the kingdom where there is currently not enough of that demonstration. In this way the alien's faith is tested. Faith is not truly tested until it is alien faith. Faith has not come to its highest level of potency until it is squeezed, and hammered, and bludgeoned and almost crucified. Faith that is not desperate will inevitably fail to reach the level of great faith. We must understand our utter need for God – our urgent necessity for being dependent upon Him – before we will verbalize to our Father our intense desire for His intervention.

Looking at the accounts of biblical heroes, we learn that desperate faith is seeking to survive in an ark you pieced together with your own hands as a flood rages and wipes out the rest of the world. Desperate faith is expecting your particular son of God's promise, the only one through whom the fullness of blessing will come, to be raised from the dead. Desperate faith is believing that a ragtag multitude of slaves can break through the hold of the greatest empire on earth and then conquer a foreign land held by enemy peoples. Desperate faith is asking that walls of a city fortress crumble before your eyes, that supernatural forces shut the mouths of lions and that you and your colleagues would saunter through the fiery flames and not be singed. Desperate faith expects supernatural deliverance in the midst of over-whelming odds.

Decades ago I attended seminary with a married couple from Vietnam who had experienced physical persecution in their home-land under a Communist government. As a local pastor, the husband was interrogated and imprisoned for two and a half years; other church leaders were also locked up.

The church, however, was quickly growing as men and women gave their lives to Christ, and 60 or 70 believers would gather early each weekday for an hour of prayer.

Fascinated and convicted by these reports, I would try to engage this introverted pastor between seminary classes to discover secrets to the persevering commitment and spiritual power these Vietnamese believers displayed. One day after a chapel service, I was again laying questions before this dear brother, and he at last turned to me and simply said, "When you're out on the high seas, and you know you're in a small boat, you depend on God."

No one accomplishes great things spiritually without great faith, desperate faith. And the life of an alien in Christ is a life of faith.

Chapter 11

An Anti-Alien Approach

O ne of my daughters, at the time a public middle school teacher, worked long after most staff had left the building. As she finally headed out on that December day, she turned a corner in a hallway to come upon the principal removing a poster featuring a nativity scene.

Earlier, a Spanish teacher and her class had placed a number of posters on a wall – but only the one with the Christian imagery was now coming down. When the principal turned and saw our daughter, knowing her biblical convictions and how his actions might look to her, he abruptly spit out profanity using the name of Jesus Christ.

When our daughter later told us this account, I wondered if the only way the name of Jesus can enter some public-school buildings in our time is as a curse word.

No matter your views on religious images in public settings, the debate as to whether our society has gotten more or less friendly toward Christianity is over. There are energetic forces seeking to dismantle fundamental expressions of the Christian faith.

We must not be shocked when the world hears the invitation

to be a spiritual alien and marches resolutely in the opposite direction. But even as we seek to thoroughly understand what it means to be an alien for God, we also do well to understand the forces that want to eliminate biblical influences in our world.

Paul spoke of this awareness when he said, regarding the enemy of our souls, that he and other Christians "are not unaware of his schemes" (2 Cor. 2:11, NIV). He also instructed us to "put on the full armor of God, so that you may be able to stand against the stratagems of the devil" (Eph. 6:11, LEB).

These schemes and stratagems are not always blatant attacks. "Satan himself is disguised as an angel of light" (2 Cor. 11:14b). Many times, the evil one is subtly removing vestiges of Christianity and stealthily nudging individuals and groups further away from biblical principles. It's important for us as disciples to recognize the patterns of anti-Christian agendas as we seek to wage not earthly warfare, but rather, to expand a heavenly kingdom. In short, for the spiritual battle that we're called to, we must know what we're up against.

Building at Babel

Mankind's track record of rebelling against God is familiar to those who follow the scriptural narrative. After Noah's Flood, humanity's resistance comes to a key juncture at a place called Babel (sometimes referred to as Babylon). Rather than fulfill God's early decree to spread out upon the earth and populate a wide variety of locations (see Gen. 1:28 and 9:1), a sizeable throng determined to join forces and seek their own transcendence:

> The whole earth had a common language and a common vocabulary. When the people moved eastward, they found a plain in Shinar and settled there. Then they said to one another, 'Come, let's make bricks and bake them thoroughly.' (They had brick instead of stone and tar instead of mortar.) Then they said,

'Come, let's build ourselves a city and a tower with its top in the heavens so that we may make a name for ourselves. Otherwise we will be scattered across the face of the entire earth.' But the Lord came down to see the city and the tower that the people had started building. And the Lord said, 'If as one people all sharing a common language they have begun to do this, then nothing they plan to do will be beyond them. Come, let's go down and confuse their language so they won't be able to understand each other.' So the Lord scattered them from there across the face of the entire earth, and they stopped building the city. That is why its name was called Babel – because there the Lord confused the language of the entire world, and from there the Lord scattered them across the face of the entire earth" (Gen. 11:1-9, NET).

With the building project at Babel, we witness human unity and initiative, but unfortunately these qualities are divorced from allegiance to the Most High. To put it another way, the early Babylonians resolutely sought to be anti-aliens, to fight for earthly preservation and prestige. They gave themselves to being rooted in a place of their choosing rather than being dependent upon the living God.

For the early Babylonians, there are three key aspects of their joining forces with each other: 1) A common language, 2) a common location, and 3) a common goal.

1. A Common Language

The passage explains that "the whole earth had a common language and a common vocabulary." The Babel builders had a shared language, the one everybody else had as well, and they used that mutual mode of communication to plan and work together. In a similar way, groups down through history, operating as entities within a broader society, have used common terminology to forward their goals.

Specialized vocabularies can be used for different reasons. For example, financial advisors, not wanting to scare investors, may choose to speak not of "stocks losing value," but of "corrections," or, when discussing the overall stock market, a "bear market."

Or terminology can be used for more nefarious purposes. The Nazi regime of the early 1900s utilized wording for specific, destructive reasons as they took control of Germany. The term *Untermenschen*, which translates as "sub-human" (literally "under people"), was a designated way to describe Jewish individuals. *Aryan* referred to a master race: Gentile, non-Gypsy Anglo, without deformities, and preferably with blond hair and blue eyes.

A German word which conveyed the idea of the "Final Solution to the Jewish 'Problem,'" was a term which really meant killing all Jews once they were within reach and the opportunity presented itself. Another German word which translated as "special treatment" was used to refer to execution.

Make no mistake, the Nazi leadership understood well the power of language and communication. Joseph Goebbels, minister of propaganda, reportedly said, "Repeat a lie often enough and it becomes the truth."

Language has frequently been used to attack one's enemies and forward one's agenda. This is seen readily in the identity politics of our time, as, for example, when voices far to the left use a litany of terms to demonize their philosophical opponents: White supremacists, Christian nationalists, the Patriarchy, proponents of toxic masculinity, etc.

Let's look at the first label I just mentioned. The problem for us today is not in calling out the evil of white supremacy. There are white supremacists in our society, and their ideology is discriminatory and ungodly. The problem here is an unwarranted expansion of the category. That is to say, some voices lump evangelical Christians in with actual white supremacists, even when they know full well that is a false grouping.

And of course, the same type of thing happens on the other end of the political spectrum, when, for example, some on the right label as Marxists anyone whose politics swings to the left.

When it comes to mislabeling, the enemies of Jesus did something similar to Him: "The scribes who had come down from Jerusalem said, 'He has Beelzebul in Him!' and, 'He drives out demons by the ruler of the demons!'" (Mk. 3:22). In their use of language, the religious leaders lumped the Son of God together with the father of lies.

Another way language is used to forward agenda is with the transgender movement. Even when we start with the word I've just mentioned, we need to consider that "transgender" conveys that an individual can actually transition from one gender to another, which, biblically and biologically, is impossible, regardless of what medical capabilities exist in our time.

Within that movement, a particularly egregious use of terminology comes with what some call "gender-affirming surgery," which of course consist of procedures that actually obfuscate gender, as medical personnel alter and even remove completely healthy, functioning body parts. When the enemy of our souls can't fit his agenda to society's thought forms, he'll change the thought forms to fit his agenda. But regardless of how much this kind of deceptive wording can mobilize masses and stir up persecution for believers, it can never truly alter the underlying reality that God has established.

What many fail to recognize is that rebellion loves to masquerade as a positive good, whether it be the Babel builders trying to construct a city or social activists trying to construct new understandings of gender.

Looking more broadly at modern terminology, we note the phrase "my personal truth," a contradiction in terms as genuine, objective truth cannot be personal. If 2 + 2 = 4, then that equation is true for both you and me, as well as everyone else. Yes, there are matters that are opinion more than fact, and there are circumstances that change over time, but when it comes to mathematics, biology and theology, as well as many other fields, there is concrete truth and falsehood, not "my personal truth" and "your personal truth."

As Christians, we have an incredible, life-giving vocabulary. One precious term in the Bible is *redeem*, to "buy back," as in God purchasing us at a slave auction where we were bound by the shackles of our own personal sin, so that He then can set us free. Another powerful word is *justification* – God declaring us legally righteous before His holy nature.

2. A Common Location

> When the people moved eastward, they found a plain in Shinar and settled there. ... Then they said, 'Come, let's build ourselves a city and a tower'" (vv. 2, 4a).

The early Babylonians directly opposed the divine mandate to spread out across the earth. Instead, they sought to centralize their efforts and consolidate their labors for the purpose of security and significance. And in this way a shared location became paramount for them.

Various groups in society utilize common locations to facilitate their plans. Considering the historical example again of the Nazis, they often met in beer halls located in Munich, Berlin and other German cities, to advance their cause. Such sites hosted a number of early, important speeches by Adolph Hitler.

Of course, the location doesn't have to involve brick and mortar. Social media serves as a virtual meeting ground for many ideologically oriented groups today.

As Christians the common location God has graciously given to us is the church of Jesus Christ. The church is our spiritual family and provides an essential home for worship, edification, fellowship, accountability and mission.

3. A Common Goal

> Then they said, 'Come, let's build ourselves a city and a tower with its top in the heavens so that we may make a name for ourselves. Otherwise, we will be scattered across the face of the entire earth'" (Gen. 11:4).

As stated previously, the Babel builders had two overarching goals: Security and significance. Security is represented by the city they were constructing, that they would not be scattered over the earth. Significance is represented by the tower they were erecting, that they would make a name for themselves.

When it comes to how we tend to look after ourselves in one way or another, these are two key motivations for mankind through history. When the serpent came to Eve in the Garden, he tempted her regarding security ("you will not die") and regarding significance ("you will be like God").

Now, we need to clarify that security and significance are not necessarily wrong to pursue. In fact, only one chapter after the Babel incident, God gives His memorable call to Abraham, saying: "I will bless you, I will make your name great" (Gen. 12:2).

First, God says that He will bless Abraham – that is to say, He will endow with power for fruitfulness. In other words, He will provide security. Additionally, God says that He will make Abraham's name great. In other words, He will provide significance.

With Babel, security and significance are coveted from below; with Abraham, however, security and significance are received from above.

Some Germans joined the Nazi regime for security, some joined for significance, and some joined for both. In our time, those adhering to leftist ideologies at times seek security in government, and seek significance in cancelling those who oppose them. Those on the political right can seek security in guns and ammunition and seek significance in having a following.

Whenever we pursue either security or significance apart from God, we fall into idolatry. For example, if I see my income as my ultimate source of provision, then I'm worshipping my income, not my Savior. If I view my spouse as my main source of contentment, then I'm worshipping my spouse, not my Redeemer. God may use various means presently as channels for His blessing, but our hearts must anchor their highest trust and devotion in the Lord, not in any earthly resource.

A phenomenally important way to ensure that our trust is in God and not in earthly resources is to praise and thank God throughout our day. This constant gratitude is necessary to set our emotions and attitudes in the right position for walking with God. This constant gratitude was most assuredly absent at Babel.

In Christ, we have genuine security: "So don't worry, saying, 'What will we eat?' or 'What will we drink?' or 'What will we wear?' ... But seek first the kingdom of God and His righteousness, and all these things will be provided for you. Therefore, don't worry about tomorrow, because tomorrow will worry about itself" (Mt. 6:31, 33-34a).

And in Christ, we have genuine significance: "Whoever wants to become great among you must be your servant, and whoever wants to be first among you must be a slave to all. For even the Son of Man did not come to be served, but to serve, and to give His life – a ransom for many" (Mk. 10:43b-45).

The Proper Pursuit

What is amazing about these words of Christ I've just quoted is: These statements directly follow the self-centered appeal of the disciples James and John to sit at the right and left of the Messiah in His glory! (see Mk. 10:35-42). Even after such a request, which immediately brought disharmony to the group of disciples, Jesus *finds nothing wrong with His followers seeking significance.* He does, however, find fault with man's pursuit of significance apart from the Lord and apart from a servant attitude.

Jesus is opposed to selfish ambition, but totally in favor of God-centered ambition. He wants us to truly thrive and prosper, but He is well aware that earthly methods to do so are, in the end, incredibly destructive. When we pursue significance in carnal ways, we fall into idolatry. Our thinking gets warped: We anticipate that dream job that will bring respect from co-workers; or that perfect spouse who will maintain my happiness; or that getaway vacation that will wash all my anxiety away. But none of these imposters for the throne of our hearts can bring eternal life, no matter how hard we try to crown them.

What we witness at Babel is God spoiling an environment where there's a common language, and in His wisdom and mercy, giving them multiple dialects. We see God spoiling a situation where there's a common location, and steering them back to His initial command, to spread out on the earth. And in this way, we see that their common goal has become unattainable – God has spoiled that as well.

They are now freed to become spiritual aliens, which is their divine call as well as ours. True, not many take Him up on that call, and so in the next chapter of Genesis, He addresses Abraham with an invitation to sojourn, as we've already seen.

At that point, God instructs the patriarch to leave familiar family and society and go to a land that He will show him.

Genesis chapters 11 and 12 leave us with a choice, the same choice that is presented to men and women throughout Scripture again and again. That choice is to either become entrenched in the ambitions and attractions of this age, like the Babylonian builders, or to be true spiritual aliens like Abraham, trusting in God, traveling the path He takes us on, and seeking to glorify Him by doing His will.

When the Spirit Moves

Fortunately for us, God did not throw in the towel after the Fall, the Flood, or the failure at Babel. He is steadfast and persevering.

Thousands of years after the Babel confusion, the Lord did have willing recipients for the offer to be spiritual aliens. I'm thinking of a specific event in Jerusalem, which serves as the corrective fulfillment to the Babel experiment:

> When the day of Pentecost arrived, they were all together in one place. And suddenly there came from heaven a sound like a mighty rushing wind, and it filled the entire house where they were sitting. And divided tongues as of fire appeared to them and rested on each one of them. And they were all filled with the Holy Spirit and began to speak in other tongues as the Spirit gave them utterance. Now there were dwelling in Jerusalem Jews, devout men from every nation under heaven. And at this sound the multitude came together, and they were bewildered, because each one was hearing them speak in his own language. And they were amazed and astonished, saying, 'Are not all these who are speaking Galileans? And how is it that we hear, each of us in his own native language?'" (Acts 2:1-9, ESV).

At times in Scripture, accounts happening earlier in history are in crucial ways fulfilled by accounts happening later. For example, the Genesis account of Abraham's willingness to offer Isaac finds a true fulfillment in the gospel accounts of Christ's crucifixion, where a Father could and would – grievingly – sacrifice his earthly Son. In a similar way, the Pentecost account serves as a genuine fulfillment to the Tower of Babel incident.

A Tale of Two Sites

It's enlightening to compare the Babel account to the Pentecost event. (In the following paragraphs, italics are used to highlight comparison and contrast between the two accounts, utilizing the ESV translation in quotations throughout.)

At Babel, "as people migrated from the east, they found a plain in the land of Shinar and *settled there*." At Jerusalem, "when

the day of Pentecost arrived, they were *all together in one place.*"
The difference, then, is this: The Babylonians gathered to settle;
the pilgrims gathered in Jerusalem to worship and (in God's sovereignty) later to, as they traveled back home, take the gospel of
Christ beyond their initial gathering spot.

Along the same lines, at Babel, they sought to combine their
talents to plant themselves in the projected city, "*lest we be
dispersed over the face of the whole earth.*" At Jerusalem, those who
came to the place of worship were "devout men *from every nation
under heaven.*"

At Babel, they proposed to build "a tower *with its top in the
heavens.*" At Pentecost, "there *came from heaven* a sound like a
mighty rushing wind, and it filled the entire house where they
were sitting." The Babylonians sought to climb up to the divine;
the pilgrims were beneficiaries of a heavenly anointing coming
down to them. It's also worth noting that in the book of Revelation, Babylon, which represents a demonized world system, is
contrasted with "the holy city, Jerusalem, *coming down out of
heaven* from God" (21:10b).

At Babel, "they said, 'Come, let us build ourselves a city and a
tower ... and *let us make a name for ourselves.*" At Jerusalem, they
said, "... we hear them *telling in our own tongues the mighty works
of God.*" The Babylonians desired to make themselves famous; the
Jewish pilgrims determined to make God famous.

At Babel, God determines to "confuse their language so that
they will not understand one another's speech." At Jerusalem, the
account states that "*each one was hearing them speak in his own
language.*" The Lord opposes self-centered pursuits, but blesses
Christ-centered pursuits.

Motivation and Direction

At Babel, men tried to build up to the heavens. At Pentecost,
heaven came down to men. At Babel, there is a unity, but it is
man-centered. At Pentecost, there is a unity, and it is God-

centered. At Babel, one language becomes many. At Pentecost, in effect, many languages become one.

The Babel account is about man's efforts to experience God-like status. The Pentecost account is about the Lord's blessing so that man can experience God.

The Genesis 11 passage is about selfish ambition: The builders at Babel wanted to make a name for themselves and not God. The Acts 2 account is about selfless reception: The worshippers at Jerusalem received power from God that they could never manufacture.

The tower of Babel account – in fact much of the book of Genesis – is about man's attempt to provide his own paradise: Adam and Eve partake of the forbidden fruit; Cain destroys the one who received the coveted divine praise; Lot chose the more promising fertile land; Joseph's brothers seek to rid themselves of the father's favorite; and of course the Babel builders attempt to establish a city and a tower to the heavens. Mankind is unwilling to accept and receive what God wisely intends for us, but reaches out to claim that which he mistakenly thinks will bring him fulfillment.

Coming into our own time, we humans are proficient at choosing what we believe is life-giving, but brings destruction to ourselves and others: We choose the entertainment we want, the luxury we want, the sexual activity we want, the gender we want. We determine that our ways are far better than God's, and then shake our fists toward the heavens when consequences eventually slap us in the face. When results of our self-indulgent choices bring decline and ruin – our resentment brings broken relationships, our illicit sex brings broken bodies – we look around for someone and something else to blame.

But when we find our significance in Christ, we are released and empowered. We are set free from the pressures and expectations of society which seek to force us into legalistic roles and regulations, always trying to get approval from others, always attempting to outdo the next person. In Christ we become free from worry, fear and pride. We only see the Lord high and lifted up, and we become fully aware that eternal life and joy evermore are found only in Him.

Forsaking the Familiar

But to experience the fullness God has in mind for us, we must leave the site of Babel. That is to say, we at times must abandon what may be extremely familiar – just as Abraham and Sarah and other biblical heroes did, each in their own time.

We're called to such alien roles in many different ways. As I was growing up and going through school, I wrestled with that call to "go to [Christ] outside the camp, bearing His disgrace" (Heb. 13:13). The high school, college and seminary I attended were all connected to my home denomination, which, tragically, was abandoning a submission and commitment to biblical authority.

One incident captures this tension pretty well. During a seminary class period, the professor was describing a spiritual conversion process for individuals that, in my estimation, was not scriptural and actually raised all kinds of red flags. I went up to him at the session break and referenced an account found in Acts 16, in which Paul the apostle has an evangelistic opportunity. "So, if you were in Paul's shoes," I asked the professor, "and the Pilippian jailer said to you, 'Sir, what must I do to be saved?' how would you respond?" (Paul's response in the account is, "Believe on the Lord Jesus, and you will be saved ...")

"Go to church," said the professor.

"How many times do I have to go to church in order to be saved?" I asked.

"You're obsessed with salvation," said my professor.

"No, I'm not," I fired back, "and my life bears witness that I'm not." (Afterward, it occurred to me that if a person is going to be obsessed with something, salvation is the correct object!)

With several professors more interested in damaging students' confidence in the Bible rather than developing it, those classrooms were no spiritual refuge for me. Sadly, despite its claim as a Christian institution, my seminary was too often foreign territory of the wrong kind for students committed to the authority of Scripture.

Sometimes, even in religious settings, we're reminded that this world is not our home.

Chapter 12

Citizens in the Next Age

When I was a young boy, my father was once visiting with an elderly man. As the two of them were finishing their conversation, the man turned to me and made an offer. "The next time I see you," he said, "if you can quote from memory Psalm 1, I will give you a dollar." This was in the early 1970s, and a dollar sounded very appealing to me. Months went by, but finally the anticipated moment came as one day I spotted the older man. I ran up to him, reminded him of the promise, and quoted Psalm 1. Smiling, he pulled a dollar from his wallet and handed it to me.

So that's how I was motivated to memorize a portion of God's word over 50 years ago. Now, I realize, at this point, some may ask, "But isn't that using material gain for spiritual pursuits?"

In response, I can say that I know three things about that memorization exercise. It was a positive experience for me, it was a positive experience for the elderly man, and the words of Psalm 1 remain in my memory banks – spanning over half a century – until this day.

It was once said, "A bribe is a prize for doing something bad. A reward is a prize for doing something good."

A Realization of Rewards

Spiritual aliens are pursuing the greatest of rewards – the prizes that are spiritual. Now when we consider the highest level of spiritual rewards, we begin delving into the subject of the next life.

And once we start thinking about what we can experience in the next life, we realize that being in the unfiltered presence of the Lord as we're ushered into the New Jerusalem is supreme. It is an unparalleled reality. That is to say, nothing compares to entering into our heavenly, permanent home and being face to face with Christ. In a familiar passage from Hebrews, we see this strong connection between spiritual aliens and the pursuit of a heavenly dwelling, where we will rest in the perfect presence of God:

> These all died in faith without having received the promises, but they saw them from a distance, greeted them, and confessed that they were foreigners and temporary residents on the earth. Now those who say such things make it clear that they are seeking a homeland. If they had been remembering that land they came from, they would have had opportunity to return. But they now aspire to a better land – a heavenly one. Therefore God is not ashamed to be called their God, for He has prepared a city for them" (Heb. 11:13-16). "For here we do not have an enduring city; instead, we seek the one to come" (Heb. 13:14).

Why did the biblical heroes seek a homeland, an enduring city, beyond this life? Why did they aspire to a better land? Because true followers of Christ have as their focus a world not lived in yet, but one they can sense in their spirits. They know that the second world is more real than the first, and they are living their lives now in anticipation of what they will receive later.

The book of Hebrews opens the door to an understanding that there are additional rewards for many of God's people: "The one who draws near to [God] must believe that He exists and rewards those who seek Him" (11:6b). And we'll see other passages testifying to this truth as we move through this chapter.

Without question, there is often confusion about eternal rewards, and much of this confusion is found within the church. Let's look at three myths regarding judgment and spiritual reward and what Scripture has to say about each one of these myths.

Myth #1 – Christians are Not Judged on Judgment Day

Many believers have this idea that coming before the throne of God means only hearing whether one goes to heaven or hell. To be clear, that does take place, and that determination is overwhelmingly the most significant outcome a person will hear regarding one's entire existence. But, to be sure, it is not the only determination for the new age:

> Then I saw a great white throne and One seated on it. Earth and heaven fled from His presence, and no place was found for them. I also saw the dead, the great and the small, standing before the throne, and books were opened. Another book was opened, which is the book of life, and the dead were judged according to their works by what was written in the books. Then the sea gave up its dead, and Death and Hades gave up their dead; all were judged according to their works. Death and Hades were thrown into the lake of fire. This is the second death, the lake of fire. And anyone not found written in the book of life was thrown into the lake of fire" (Rev. 20:11-15).

John describes the foundational judgment of whether an individual goes to the New Jerusalem or the lake of fire. This decision is recorded in the book of life, which is mentioned in verse 12 above. We also read the following in verse 15: "And anyone not found written in the book of life was thrown into the lake of fire."

But there's more: "I also saw the dead, the great and the small, standing before the throne, and books were opened. ... and the dead were judged according to their works by what was written in the books. ... all were judged according to their works" (Rev. 20:12a, 12c, 13b).

This teaching that all will be judged according to their works is repeated numerous times in Scripture, and the Word of God clarifies that this judgment is for believers as well as unbelievers. Paul writes to the Christians at Corinth: "Therefore, whether we are at home or away, we make it our aim to be pleasing to Him. For we must all appear before the judgment seat of Christ, so that each may be repaid for what he has done in the body, whether good or bad" (2 Cor. 5:9-10).

Remember what the writer of Hebrews said about that spiritual alien Moses: "For he considered reproach for the sake of the Messiah to be greater wealth than the treasures of Egypt, since his attention was on the reward" (Heb. 11:26).

Moses might have had every earthly reason to focus on the treasures of Egypt – he was raised by Pharoah's daughter – but he was looking for eternal reward.

As said previously, of course the greatest reality we will experience in the next life is first and foremost being with the Lord. But being face to face with Christ doesn't rule out various rewards He offers, such as, for example, some of the crowns mentioned in the New Testament.

In chapters five and six of Matthew, the word "reward" (both noun and verb) is used in many translations no fewer than nine times. These chapters teach Christlike ethics in the foundational message that we call the Sermon on the Mount. In other words, when Jesus instructs His followers in how to live, He motivates them by speaking of reward from God. For example: "Blessed are you when they insult you and persecute you and falsely say every kind of evil against you because of Me. Be glad and rejoice, because your reward is great in heaven" (Mt. 5:11-12a).

Christ wants us to clearly understand that how we live now affects our eternity.

Myth #2 – All Christians Receive the Same Reward for Eternity

While some Christians think that fairness entails that there is no judgment of our works, other Christians believe that followers of Christ all receive the same judgment. The conclusion many come to is that God should treat all his followers exactly the same. But the Lord, on a regular basis, treats his followers differently. Look at creation – the very first two individuals God created had different genders, different roles and different functions!

And this pattern of God making each person unique continues into our time. For example, God creates us with vastly different skill sets – I certainly don't have the athletic ability of LeBron James or the mathematical aptitude of Albert Einstein. Yet I can worship, obey and serve God with whatever capacity I do possess. And with His comprehensive and perfect knowledge, God is certainly able and prepared to judge us based on what we've done with what we've been given. His grace in multiple forms – the unmerited favor of saving grace, as well as the divine enablement of empowering grace – is available to each individual. Thus, we are responsible for how we utilize what the Lord has made accessible to us.

> For if the eagerness is there, [a believer's gift] is acceptable according to what one has, not according to what he does not have" (2 Cor. 8:12).

Paul speaks in the following passage particularly about Christian leaders, but the principles he shares certainly apply to all believers:

> Now the one who plants and the one who waters are equal, and each will receive his own reward according to his own labor. ... no one can lay any other foundation than what has been laid – that is, Jesus Christ. If anyone builds on the foundation with

gold, silver, costly stones, wood, hay, or straw, each one's work will become obvious, for the day will disclose it, because it will be revealed by fire; the fire will test the quality of each one's work. If anyone's work that he has built survives, he will receive a reward. If anyone's work is burned up, it will be lost, but he will be saved; yet it will be like an escape through fire" (1 Cor. 3:8, 11-15).

For thousands of years metals have been tested by fire, and in similar fashion God will test our effort and commitment when it comes to doing the Lord's will. Some, who do make it to glory, will nevertheless have their "work ... burned up" while others, ministering sacrificially and with a commitment to excellence, will be rewarded greatly by the Most High.

Paul is simply continuing the doctrine that Christ Himself set forth in clear language: "For the Son of Man is going to come with His angels in the glory of His Father, and then He will reward each according to what he has done" (Mt. 16:27). And these are Jesus' words recorded at the end of the Bible: "Look! I am coming quickly, and My reward is with Me to repay each person according to what he has done" (Rev. 22:12).

How do we find a balance? We can easily fall into one extreme or the other when it comes to different rewards for different people. And in this case organized sports gives us analogies that demonstrate both extremes. At one extreme is the framework for many children's athletic events, where each child gets a participation trophy and nothing more, no matter how poorly or how well that child competed. But this would-be analogy doesn't work with Christian discipleship, because various believers will receive different levels of rewards.

At the other extreme in the United States is professional sports, where the emotional and psychological well-being of fans rests on how well their team did in its last contest – and even on how strong the statistics were compiled by their favorite players. Fans spend exorbitant amounts of money on tickets, team gear and accessories and, especially, gambling. Some even, as they consider their earthly mortality, insist on listing their love of team in their obituaries.

So this latter sports example, this full-blown devotion to one's favorite team, also falls woefully short as a metaphor when it comes to the kingdom of God. In pro sports – in contrast to how the Lord treats His disciples – one team out of the entire pack rises to the summit and takes the title, while every other team is defeated at one stage or the other.

THE WAY GOD HAS ESTABLISHED THINGS, WHEN WE pursue Christ and earn greater eternal reward, the same will often be true for others around us. For example, if I study Scripture diligently and teach the Word accurately and passionately, invariably some listening will be inspired to follow the Lord more resolutely. If I serve the church with devotion and joy, invariably others will be motivated to do the same. We will not compete, but collaborate.

From a worldly point of view, with our rivalries, we frequently compare ourselves to others and seek to climb over them so as to come out on top. In Christianity, we compare ourselves only to Christ, which should always leave us thankful and humble – thankful that a spotless Lamb was willing to go to the Cross, and humble that even though I fall so short of His standard, God has welcomed me into His own blessed family, through Jesus.

The road to spiritual reward and the road to selfless Christlikeness *are the exact same path*. Often when many of us think of any kind of gain, we think of stepping on and then over someone else to acquire the reward. With the way of Jesus, this is exactly the opposite: To gain spiritually, we help others move forward. Do we not perceive this principle when we read Christ's teaching of the sheep and the goats?

> Then the King will say to those on His right, 'Come, you who are blessed by My Father, inherit the kingdom prepared for you from the foundation of the world. For I was hungry and you gave Me something to eat; I was thirsty and you gave Me something to drink; I was a stranger and you took Me in; I was naked and you clothed Me; I was sick and you took care of Me; I was in prison and you visited Me.'
>
> Then the righteous will answer Him, 'Lord, when did we see You hungry and feed You, or thirsty and give You something to drink? When did we see You a stranger and take You in, or without clothes and clothe You? When did we see You sick, or in prison, and visit You?' And the King will answer them, 'I assure you: Whatever you did for one of the least of these brothers of Mine, you did for Me'" (Mt. 25:34-40).

Another factor in this discussion is that, undoubtedly, many Christians don't want to confront the reality that their day-to-day decisions have eternal consequences. That is to say, our seemingly small actions, thoughts, attitudes and words will frequently bring us either approval or disapproval from an all-powerful, all-knowing, completely holy God. This is a sobering truth that many like to hopefully keep on a back shelf somewhere out of sight. But the reality remains, and we do well to meditate upon it and apply it to our lives.

Myth #3 – Christians are Not to Seek Any Reward

Another angle on the issue of believers and reward is the approach: "I am not seeking any eternal rewards. I'm just living to please God out of the goodness of my heart."

In these cases, one should carefully evaluate the state of his or her moral condition. Here's what Scripture says: "The heart is more deceitful than anything else and desperately sick – who can understand it?" (Jer. 17:9). This verse reminds us of the thrust of Chapter 2: Alienated from God. That is to say, we are often more evil than we think we are.

We may be tempted to proclaim, "Well, I don't need eternal rewards because I will just do the right thing because it's the right thing." But if so, are we not fooling ourselves about how inherently moral, undefiled and perfected we're assuming we've become?

God came to save and empower sinners, not spiritually wonderful and flawless people. Jesus said to His early listeners: "For if you love those who love you, what reward will you have?" (Mt. 5:46a). That is to say, He clearly offered reward for obeying His will. He used reward to motivate His hearers.

Even once we've become believers in Jesus, we still struggle against a sinful nature that resides within us. This is why we're taught to pray to God on a regular basis "forgive us our debts" (Mt. 6:12a). "All have turned away, together they have become useless; there is no one who does good, there is not even one" (Rom. 3:12). As James says to his Christian readers: "we all stumble in many ways" (3:2a).

God calls us to fight the good fight, and to battle against principalities and powers of this dark age in overcoming evil. And He is pleased to reward His followers who make use of His grace in order to advance the kingdom of God.

The kingdom of darkness will continue to stand against us, and will take advantage of original sin, and continuing sin, to oppose Christ's agenda. But the Lord values His children's genuine attempts to display the attributes of His kingdom, and He delights in bestowing rewards upon us as we enter into the new age. "Watch yourselves so that you don't lose what we have worked for, but you may receive a full reward" (2 Jn. v. 8).

The Lesson of Love

Some seem to find the concept of spiritual rewards cold and mechanical, but notice what Paul said in the classic 1 Corinthians 13 love chapter: "And if I donate all my goods to feed the poor, and if I give my body to be burned, but do not have love, *I gain nothing*" (v. 3, emphasis added). Rewards have everything to do with love! If there is no love, there is no reward from the God who is love.

Are you living a life of love in Christ? Are you living a life that will incur significant reward? If you're not sure, I would encourage you to do an extensive biblical study on eternal rewards. There is a wealth of material to cover in Scripture regarding spiritual rewards, and such a study will be – well, rewarding!

Spiritual aliens are pursuing spiritual rewards. And they realize that the greatest rewards are not to be found in this life. Their gaze is a bit beyond the horizon. They're thankful for earthly comforts of friends and family, of hearth and home, of sunrises and new seasons, but their genuine delight is altogether in another realm.

The Source of Our Satisfaction

The story is told of an elderly missionary couple, over a century ago, sailing into their home port after years of faithful but difficult service in Africa. They had no pension and their health was weak. To tell the truth, they were somewhat discouraged and uncertain about the future.

As their ship drew close to the harbor, expectations of fanfare were completely absent from their minds. Imagine their surprise, then, as they came closer to the dock and heard a rising roar. They saw a large crowd gathered. A band was playing with gusto and newspapermen were taking pictures.

But as it turns out, the fanfare had nothing to do with them.

An American ambassador and his wife, unknown to the missionary couple, had traveled on the same ship and were greeted with a hero's welcome. Roses were bestowed upon the glamorous wife and the press and public hung on every word given by the high-ranking official as he spoke about the joy of serving overseas and now coming home.

The missionary couple meekly made their way unnoticed through the crowd and the godly wife, processing everything and weary from the trip, finally reached her breaking point. With hot tears streaming down her cheeks, she turned and said in a low but intense whisper to her husband, "Why is it that we have given our whole lives to Christ and yet there is not a single person here to honor us and welcome us home?"

Her husband was silent for a long moment. But then a tranquil spirit swept over him and the path seemed a little less murky. He leaned over his wife and whispered in her ear, "But honey, you and I are not yet home."

There Is Jesus

1. There are trou - bles coming to us, O - ver-whelm us, and we stum-ble on our way.
2. Oth - ers leave us or de-ceive us; All these strug-gles our Mes-si - ah knew so well.
3. Though we fal - ter, we are ris - ing; Al-ways seek-ing, as we put our trust in Him.

Hope goes miss-ing, we are wish-ing For an an-swer that will lead to bright-er day.
And He of - fers to re-lieve us, And with-in us, Je-sus Christ has come to dwell.
Grace will move us, truth will prove us. God is ho - ly, and He cleans-es us from sin.

God is a - ble! He is might - y; By His Spir-it He will come up-on our lives.
There's a prom-ise, ev-er faith - ful, Nev-er fail-ing, that will bring us out of night.
God is a - ble! He is might - y; By His Spir-it He will come up-on our lives.
There's a prom-ise, ev-er faith - ful, Nev-er fail-ing, that will bring us out of night.

Through the de-sert, through the fire, We are giv-en what we need in Him to thrive.
There is Je-sus, lov-ing Full - ness, Per-fect Shep-herd, who will lead us to the light.
Through the de-sert, through the fire, We are giv-en what we need in Him to thrive.
There is Je-sus, lov-ing Full - ness, Per-fect Shep-herd, who will lead us to the light.

Music & Lyrics: Daryl Driver, 2024 © 2024, info@wordofgracepa.com

About the Author

The career and ministry path of Daryl Driver has included pastoral leadership, Bible college teaching, newspaper journalism and serving on multiple church-related boards. He is currently pastor of Word of Grace Church, Lancaster, PA, a congregation he helped launch; overseer for several other congregations; and executive board member for the Rosedale Network of Churches. He finds New Testament disciple-making to be challenging but rewarding, and also enjoys spending time with family, talking with a variety of people about religion and reality, and following national and world news and trends. Daryl and his wife Kay are greatly blessed to have five children and three grandchildren.

For more about the book, go to wordofgracepa.com/book-alien

Reach the author at info@wordofgracepa.com